FRENCH DRAWINGS

FRENCH DRAWINGS

from the

National Gallery

of Canada

Sonia Couturier

Ottawa

2004

The exhibition

French Drawings from the National Gallery of Canada

is organized and circulated by the National Gallery of Canada.

ITINERARY

National Gallery of Canada

21 May – 29 August 2004

Art Gallery of Greater Victoria

4 December 2004 – 20 February 2005

Edmonton Art Gallery

16 September – 17 November 2005

NATIONAL GALLERY OF CANADA
Chief, Publications Division: Serge Thériault
Editors: Lynda Muir and Denise Sirois
Picture Editor: Colleen Evans
Translation: Marcia L. Barr and Marcia Couëlle

Printed in Canada

NATIONAL LIBRARY OF CANADA CATALOGUING IN PUBLICATION DATA

National Gallery of Canada.
French drawings from the National Gallery of Canada / Sonia Couturier.

Exhibition catalogue.
Issued also in French under title: Dessins français du Musée des beaux-arts du Canada
ISBN 0-88884-781-5

1. Drawing, French–Exhibitions. 2. Drawing–Ontario–Ottawa–Exhibitions.
3. National Gallery of Canada–Exhibitions. I. Couturier, Sonia, 1969– . II. Title.

NC246 N38 2004   741.944'074'71384   C2004-986001-3

Available through your local bookseller or from:
The Bookstore
National Gallery of Canada
380 Sussex Drive, Box 427, Station A, Ottawa KIN 9N4

FRONT COVER
Charles de La Fosse, *Study of Nestor and His Associates, after Peter Paul Rubens* (cat. 11)
BACK COVER
Jacques Louis David, *Portrait Assumed to be of Jean-Baptiste Robert Lindet* (cat. 43)

Designed and typeset by Expression Communications Inc.
Typeset in Centaur
Printed on acid-free paper
Printed by Tri-Graphic Printing (Ottawa) Limited

Contents

FOREWORD

The impressive corpus of works on paper in the collection of the National Gallery of Canada comprises one of the treasures of our national heritage. Following the two earlier exhibitions that featured Italian drawings and Dutch and Flemish drawings from our permanent collection, this new show brings together seventy of the most beautiful sheets in our holdings from the French school of the seventeenth, eighteenth, and nineteenth centuries. Drawing is one of the foundations of French art, and presenting these works together serves to illuminate the richness of this form of artistic expression, and its dominant characteristics.

This publication is the third in a series intended to introduce our collection of prints and drawings. The catalogue provides an opportunity to discover some sheets that have never been published before, and positions our collection of French drawings among the most significant in North America. I would like to stress the outstanding contribution of Sonia Couturier, Assistant Curator of Prints and Drawings, who selected the works to be displayed and wrote the catalogue.

I would also like to thank Sotheby's Canada for its sponsorship of this project, and express our gratitude to the museums who will be hosting the exhibition.

Pierre Théberge, O.C., C.Q.
Director
National Gallery of Canada

ACKNOWLEDGMENTS

This catalogue owes its existence to the support and confidence shown to me by Pierre Théberge, Director of the National Gallery of Canada, and by David Franklin, Chief Curator, to whom I am most grateful. I would like to underscore the contribution of research assistants Muriel Clair and Marie-Christine Beaudry, whose diligence and passion for their work were exemplary. I would also like to express my appreciation to Denise Sirois and Lynda Muir for their meticulous editing, and my gratitude to Anne Maheux and Geoffrey Morrow, conservators of works on paper, for enlightening me about various aspects of conservation and advising me on the delicate handling required by some of the drawings. At every stage in the production of this catalogue, I enjoyed the support of my colleagues at the Gallery, in particular Daniel Amadei, Raven Amiro, Lucille Banville, John Barton, Chris Baxter, Joanne Beglo, Shawn Boisvert, Karen Colby-Stothart, Nelda Damiano, Pamela Osler-Delworth, Paul Elter, Colleen Evans, Julie Hodgson, Charles Hupé, Catherine Johnston, Anna Kindl-Coaker, Joseph Lakkis, Steve McNeil, Michael Pantazzi, Mark Paradis, Greg Spurgeon, Yves Théoret, Serge Thériault, Martina Todd, Peter Trepanier, and Karen Wyatt; and designer Miriam Bloom of Expression Communications. I would also like to pay tribute to the generosity of a number of experts from other institutions who gave me their unstinting aid and counsel: Elena Apostolova, Colin Bailey, Joseph Baillio, Diederik Bakhuÿs, Laura Bennett, Susanna Caviglia-Brunel, Alvin L. Clark, Marie-Anne Dupuy-Vachey, Michel-Witold Gierzod, Clémentine Gustin-Gomez, Jeffrey E. Horvitz, Lee Johnson, Françoise Joulie, Christophe Leribault, Suzanne Folds McCullagh, Jean-François Méjanès, Edgar Munhall, Madeleine Pinault-Sørensen, Christophe de Quénetain, Sue Welsh Reed, Lutz Riester, Hélène Rihal, Marianne Roland Michel, Pierre Rosenberg, and Arlette Sérullaz. I am also endebted to the museums that allowed me access to their collections, and to the devoted staff of these institutions, which include the Agnes Etherington Art Centre, Kingston, the Albertina, Vienna, the Art Gallery of Ontario, Toronto, the Art Institute of

Chicago, the Musée des Augustins, Toulouse, Musée des Beaux-Arts et d'Archéologie de Besançon, Musée Bonnat, Bayonne, the Museum of Fine Arts Boston, Musée Paul-Dupuy, Toulouse, Musée Calvet, Avignon, Musée Raymond-Lafage, Lisle-sur-Tarn, Département des arts graphiques du Musée du Louvre, Paris, the Metropolitan Museum of Art, New York, and the Musée des Beaux-Arts de Rouen. I cannot conclude these acknowledgments without expressing my gratitude to Melih Argun for his patience, and most especially to my son, Gabriel, to whom I dedicate this work.

Sonia Couturier
Assistant Curator, European and American Prints and Drawings
National Gallery of Canada

INTRODUCTION

This catalogue highlights seventy key works from the French drawings collection of the National Gallery of Canada, which consists of more than 250 sheets produced before the twentieth century. A major component of the Gallery's collection of works on paper, the holding of French drawings grew along much the same lines as that of Italian drawings presented in the inaugural catalogue in this series begun by David Franklin, Chief Curator of Prints and Drawings. The first French sheet, an *Ecce Homo* by Raymond de La Fage (cat. 12), was part of the initial core of drawings, a lot from the collection of the Duke of Rutland purchased by the Gallery in 1911. Over the years since then, a succession of advisors and curators – Paul Oppé, Arthur Ewart Popham, Kathleen Fenwick, Mimi Cazort, and David Franklin – has sought to enhance the French collection through the acquisition of outstanding works. Their purchases made with government funds have been augmented by generous gifts.

This collection, although primarily noteworthy for its many exceptional pieces, offers a panorama of the different movements that mark the history of French art from the dawn of the seventeenth century through to the late nineteenth. As well, the great variety of techniques and materials found in these examples invites an exploration of the many facets of the art of drawing. The collection ranges from sketches to finished works, in forms as different as historical and religious representations, landscapes, portraits, and genre scenes, and each of these aspects is discussed here in chronological order. The catalogue is organized by theme, but loosely enough in terms of both chronology and style to accommodate the work of artists whose influence was felt in more than one area and over several centuries. For example, the "drawn portraits" of Daniel Dumonstier (cat. 4) and Nicolas Lagneau (cat. 5) from the first half of the seventeenth century reflect the work of portraitists of the previous century, such as François Clouet. From the eighteenth century, the art of François Boucher admirably illustrates a convergence of genres: the academic tradition, apparent in those works inspired by Italian masters of the

High Baroque (cat. 20) and in his interpretations of the Old Testament (cat. 19); and the choice of lighter subjects (cat. 34 and 35) and themes adapted for decorative purposes (cat. 36).

Most of the artists presented in the first section were active prior to the founding of the Académie royale de peinture et de sculpture in 1648, or practised outside that circle. Others, such as Claude Lorrain (cat. 6 and 7), served as reference points for the emerging generation or, like Jean Cotelle I (cat. 9), were among the Académie's founding members. With the exception of Lagneau and Dumonstier, these artists, to varying degrees, clearly demonstrate the predominance of the Italian model. For example, Gaspard Dughet (cat. 8), a contemporary of Lorrain, quite literally imitated Salvator Rosa. The work of Jacques Callot, who like Jacques Bellange (cat. 1) is identified with the Lorraine school, would bear lifelong traces of his early stay at the Medici court. During his time in Florence, Callot discovered commedia dell'arte theatre, the inspiration for one of his most famous series, *Balli di Sfessania*, for which the Gallery possesses a sheet of early sketches (cat. 2). Bellange was clearly imbued with the prevailing Mannerism fostered by the Fontainebleau school; it is less certain that he travelled in Italy, although his work is reminiscent of Parmigianino in certain ways. As for Guillaume Courtois, who settled permanently in Rome with his brother Jacques while still a boy, the dynamic compositional drawing *Saint Michael Vanquishing Satan* (fig. 1) reveals the obvious influence of the work of Guido Reni at the Roman church of Santa Maria della Concezione. This sheet, classified as part of the Italian drawing collection of the National Gallery of Canada, has a counterpart in a sketch formerly ascribed to Ludovico Gimignani held in the Calcografia Nazionale in Rome.

The fecund Italian model served as the basis for the institutionalization of art in France in the 1650s and beyond, into the 1800s. The artistic doctrine was first embodied in the art of Charles Le Brun (cat. 10), whose youthful works attest the influence of Simon Vouet. Yet the Académie, for all its imposed dogma, was the subject of controversy and questioning; until the early 1700s, the inner sanctum

FIG 1 Guillaume Courtois, *Saint Michael Vanquishing Satan*, NGC

was shaken by an aesthetic debate between the proponents of Poussin's classicism, who argued that drawing is the basis of art, and the followers of Rubens, who insisted on the supremacy of colour. One member of the latter group was Charles de La Fosse, whose large drawing (cat. 11) is a copy *aux trois crayons* of a detail after the Flemish master. The younger Antoine Coypel (cat. 14) shared La Fosse's allegiance, yet he freely drew on the work of the Bolognese Annibale Carracci and later turned to Correggio in shaping compositions on themes of romantic mythology (cat. 15).

The various stages of Academic training, which focused primarily on the teaching of drawing – Old Master imitations, studies after antique sculpture, and live models – need not be reviewed here, but the pre-eminence of history painting in the hierarchy of genres must be noted. Compositions by Jean-Baptiste Corneille (cat. 13), Pierre-Jacques Cazes (cat. 16 and 17), and Charles-Joseph Natoire (cat. 22) are eloquent examples of the treatment of themes drawn from religious history and mythology. Jean-Honoré Fragonard breathed new life into the genre, both in his innovative rendering of antique reliefs (cat. 23) and in his illustrations for modern (i.e. Renaissance) literary works, among them Ariosto's *Orlando Furioso* (cat. 24). Charles Parrocel's dynamic composition (cat. 18) is in a class of its own, with the artist carrying on the battle scene tradition handed down by his father, while incorporating time-honoured motifs from the engravings of Pietro Testa. Midway between idealization and archaeology, the architectural views of Jean-Baptiste Lallemand (cat. 25), Charles-Louis Clérisseau (cat. 26), and Hubert Robert (cat. 28) demonstrate the impact of the discoveries at Pompeii and Herculaneum on the perception of Antiquity among artists of the latter 1700s. These finds would contribute to the rise of Neoclassicism, as discussed below.

Coinciding with an artistic practice that toed the official line was a movement that reflected the tastes and preferences of collectors and private patrons. A figure study for *Meeting in the Open Air* by Jean-Antoine Watteau (cat. 30) demonstrates the finesse that made him the master of the *fête galante*, and which his successors – Nicolas Lancret (cat. 32) and Pierre-Antoine Quillard (cat. 33),

among others – vainly tried to reproduce. However, the simultaneously highly refined and scenic nature of Watteau's work derives from another, lesser-known artist, Claude Gillot. Although trained as a decorative painter by his father, Gillot went beyond mere ornamentation, borrowing frequently from the Italian theatrical repertoire and occasionally from the Flemish picturesque landscape tradition (cat. 31).

In the course of the eighteenth century, the repertoire of forms changed as sensitivities and subjects came into and out of vogue, and it was in this fluctuating context that the young François Boucher developed a pastoral art (cat. 34) that would secure his rise to prominence. Boucher's student Jean-Baptiste Huet, who also trained under Le Prince (cat. 41), earned a reputation as an animal painter, and the style of his master Boucher is at times discernible in the rendering and form of his drawings (cat. 42). This same context saw the flourishing of a romantic imagery sprinkled with erotic allusions, as in Pierre-Antoine Baudouin's *Bringing the Bride to Bed* (cat. 37), which rubbed shoulders with the highly moral scenes of Jean-Baptiste Greuze. A wash composition by Greuze entitled *Return of the Traveller* (fig. 2) illustrates a new way of representing the pathos the artist expressed in early works from his stay in Rome, such as *The Neapolitan Gesture* (cat. 40), shown at the Salon of 1757. Some years before, a similar spirit of morality had suffused Jean-Baptiste Oudry's illustrations for La Fontaine's *Fables* (cat. 38); these tales later enjoyed wide distribution in the edition featuring engravings executed under the direction of Charles-Nicolas Cochin (cat. 39).

A new interest in classical antiquity grew up after 1750, reaching full flower with the French Revolution. *Portrait Assumed to be of Jean-Baptiste Robert Lindet* (cat. 43) by Jacques Louis David is notable first and foremost for its expression of Neoclassical rectitude, rooted in the ideal of *exemplum virtutis*. Jean-Baptiste-Joseph Wicar, a pupil of David, imparted the same quality to his drawn portraits of the notables with whom he kept company in Rome (cat. 45), yet they are tinged with a sentimentality that also marks the work of the portraitist Jacques-Antoine-Marie Lemoine (cat. 44), who had trained under Quentin de

FIG 2 Jean-Baptiste Greuze, *Return of the Traveller*, NGC

La Tour. Another facet in the development of Neoclassicism is history painting, which held pride of place at the Académie. While it was permissible to represent modern history, as in the composition attributed to François-Louis-Joseph Watteau (cat. 46), the principal characteristic of this movement was a fresh approach to interpreting classical texts. In accord with this trend, Jean Auguste Dominique Ingres reprised a composition executed several decades earlier, resulting in different versions of an episode of the *Aeneid* (cat. 48).

In his preparatory drawing of Atala's death (cat. 47) for the famous painting *The Funeral of Atala*, in the Louvre, Anne-Louis Girodet de Roucy-Trioson adopts the discourse of his contemporary and friend Chateaubriand to articulate his political views under the Bonaparte regime. The idealized exoticism of this painting, which is set in the Louisiana forest, prefigures the interest that other artists would take in subjects of a foreign nature. Jean-Léon Gérôme did so in almost documentary tone during his travels, as in Egypt, where he garnered the images that led to his *Donkey Driver in Cairo* (cat. 54). However, Romanticism found its fullest expression with Théodore Géricault who, in preparation for the Prix de Rome, translated his classical influences with a spirited pen (cat. 49).

Ferdinand-Victor-Eugène Delacroix achieves the same dramatic intensity in *The Barque of Dante* (cat. 50); of greater interest, though, is the mystical dimension found in Delacroix's religious pictures, especially the Crucifixions, one of which, a touching pastel (cat. 51), is in our collection.

The richly diverse nineteenth century brought myriad means of pictorial expression. Less bound to the pictorial and iconographic tradition of previous centuries, this period is notable chiefly for innovative subject matter. Gustave Courbet's realism takes an unexpected turn in the drawing of a pantomime entitled *The Black Arm* (cat. 55). Contemporary literature – poetry, in particular – and illustration conjoined with increasing frequency. Towards the end of his life, Gustave Christophe Paul Doré made a series of drawings to illustrate an original English edition of Edgar Allan Poe's poem *The Raven* (cat. 58), which became immensely popular in France in a translation by Mallarmé. Odilon Redon turned his hand to interpreting the same subject in the early 1880s (cat. 59), but he would wax most lyrical in multiple drawn and engraved versions of the myth of Pegasus (cat. 60). Gustave Moreau's poetic inspiration found embodiment in *Hesiod and the Muse* (cat. 56), a work lit by a singular spirituality, which hints at reconciliation with the forms of the

Italian Renaissance. Early works by Edgar Degas such as *Alexander and Bucephalus* (cat. 65) bear similar witness to this attempt to revisit the classical repertory, no doubt owing to the friendship the two men enjoyed while in Italy.

No discussion of the nineteenth century would be complete without mentioning the contribution of artists who cast a critical, or complaisant, eye on the society in which they lived. *Three Judges at a Hearing* (cat. 69) by Honoré Daumier superbly evokes the thriving art of caricature, which was widely circulated in the form of lithographs. Conversely, Jacques-Joseph Tissot's elegant ladies (cat. 68) were prized by the political elite who frequented the official Salons, that is, until the French painter fled to England. Informal scenes also abounded in the 1800s: the young Henri de Toulouse-Lautrec made several portraits of members of his family (cat. 66), and Pierre-Auguste Renoir opened a window onto his private life with portraits of his son Jean and his maid Gabrielle (cat. 67). During the same period, Jean-Baptiste Camille Corot spurred a revival of landscape art, taking inspiration from Claude Lorrain's classical landscapes and advocating studies direct from nature (cat. 61). Charles-François Daubigny eschewed details in favour of exploratory *plein air* painting, in an attempt to render the ever-changing face of the natural world (cat. 62). Similarly, though in different manners, Camille Pissarro (cat. 63) and Paul Cézanne (cat. 64) engaged in landscape, less as a means of representing a specific place than as a pretext for experimenting with form – and even plasticity. In the same context, but unique unto itself, was the art of Puvis de Chavannes (cat. 57), the herald of Symbolism and of an avant-garde that saw salvation in integrated disciplines. At the dawn of the twentieth century, where this survey ends, this same spirit guided a young Nabi, Pierre Bonnard, as he created his first posters (cat. 70).

CATALOGUE

NOTE TO THE READER

Unless otherwise indicated, the drawings are on laid paper.
The abbreviation "L." refers to F. Lugt, *Les Marques de collections de dessins et d'estampes*, Amsterdam, 1921; supplement,
The Hague, 1956. The number of bibliographic references has been reduced to save space. Other references can
be found in the following publications:

A.E. Popham and K.M. Fenwick, *European Drawings in the
Collection of the National Gallery of Canada*, Toronto, 1965.

Mary Cazort Taylor, ed., *European Drawings from the National
Gallery of Canada*, exh. cat., P. & D. Colnaghi, London, 1969.

*Da Dürer a Picasso. Mostra di Disegni della Galleria nazionale del
Canada*, exh. cat., Galerie des Offices, Florence, 1969.

De Raphaël à Picasso. Dessins de la Galerie nationale du Canada,
exh. cat, Musée du Louvre, Paris, 1970.

The 17th Century

Italian Influence and Northern Spirit

I

JACQUES BELLANGE

Bassigny c. 1575–1616 Nancy

Saint John the Baptist Preaching c. 1616

Black chalk, pen and brown ink
with red-brown wash, 29.9 × 31.9 cm
PURCHASED 1969

NO. 15770

PROVENANCE
Benno Geiger collection, Rodaun
(Vienna), 19th century; C. Fairfax
Murray collection, London; E.
Parsons and Sons, London; Dr.
Ludwig Burchard, 1953; Faerber and
Maison, London.

This rare black chalk and wash drawing stands alone in the drawn oeuvre of Jacques Bellange. The outlines traced with a stylus suggest that the sheet was transferred, but the composition is found neither among the artist's etchings nor among his paintings.

Saint John the Baptist Preaching exhibits certain formal characteristics typical of Late Mannerism: the high-angle perspective and the dynamic relationship between the different planes. The secondary figures in the foreground, pictured half-length from the back, serve as a counterpoint. Centred in the upper area of the composition, the figure of John the Baptist is highly theatrical, one hand raised in a declamatory gesture, the other holding a staff. Thuillier sees this scene as representing a passage from the Gospel of John (John 1:35–42), in which John the Baptist, upon espying Jesus (presumably at right, towards the back), declared, "Behold, the Lamb of God," inspiring Andrew and another disciple to follow Christ.[1]

On stylistic grounds, scholars date this sheet to the end of the artist's career.[2] Late works by Bellange akin to the National Gallery of Canada drawing include *The Raising of Lazarus* (fig. 3), considered to be one of his final etchings. Both works feature the same dense composition organized around a central figure and the same simplified draperies, which lend an air of solemnity. Also, as in the red chalk *Study of a Woman* (fig. 4),[3] Bellange has opted for sparse means and a direct approach. The resulting restrained forms are a far cry from the sinuous and elongated figures in expressive poses that distinguish the virtuoso Mannerism of his younger years.

FIG 3 Jacques Bellange, *The Raising of Lazarus*, Bibliothèque nationale, Paris

FIG 4 Jacques Bellange, *Study of a Woman*, École nationale supérieure des beaux-arts, Paris

2

JACQUES CALLOT
Nancy 1592–1635 Nancy

Figure Studies Based on Commedia dell'arte Characters VERSO: *Sketch of an Escutcheon for the Funeral Ceremonies of Margaret of Austria, Queen of Spain* c. 1612–16

Pen and brown ink, 15 × 12.7 cm
PURCHASED 1984
NO. 28440
PROVENANCE
Private collection, France; Bernard Houthakker, Amsterdam.

This sheet dates to Jacques Callot's early years in Florence, where he developed the motifs later used in *Balli di Sfessania*, a series of twenty-four etchings inspired by the commedia dell'arte and executed after his return to Nancy in 1621.[1] Certainly, the many extant preliminary drawings were produced between 1615 and 1617 in Florence, where he could observe strolling players in performance. While the Ottawa drawing does share the elegance and nervous strokes that characterize the etchings, unlike the other studies that are mainly in red chalk,[2] it does not relate directly to any one print, but rather represents initial thinking for the series. Some of the figures in the Ottawa drawing are recognizably similar to those in five sheets of the series that depict male and female characters in various poses (fig. 5).[3]

The sketch on the verso is doubtless the earliest known drawing by the Lorraine master. Topped by a death's-head and bearing the inscription *"Imprese"* in the centre field, this escutcheon points to another facet of the artist's early career: his work with the Florentine painter and engraver Antonio Tempesta. In 1612, Callot collaborated with Tempesta and Raffaello Schiaminossi on a suite of twenty-nine etchings published with a text by Giovanni Altoviti to commemorate the funeral of Margaret of Austria, Queen of Spain, wife of Philippe III and sister-in-law of Grand Duke Cosimo II.[4] This memorial commission was to pave the way for the close ties Callot enjoyed with the Medici court. The sovereign's funeral took place on 6 February 1612 at San Lorenzo di Firenze, the Medici family church, and was staged by the scenic designer Giulio Parigi. The decoration included a series of twenty-six grisaille paintings by Jacopo da Empoli illustrating the life and death of the queen. Hung along the side walls of the church, these paintings served as models for Callot's etchings. His illustration of one of the aisles (fig. 6) shows an elaborate architectural arrangement adorned with skulls, human skeletons, and heavy drapings.[5] Each column is surmounted by an armorial escutcheon (detail, fig. 6) similar in form to that of the Ottawa drawing.

FIG 5 Jacques Callot, *Riciulina and Mezzetino*, NGC

FIG 6 Jacques Callot, *A Side Aisle of the Church of San Lorenzo in Florence*, Albertina, Vienna

DETAIL (fig. 6) Armorial escutcheon

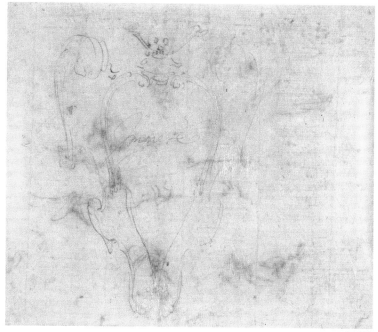

3

STUDIO OF JACQUES CALLOT
Nancy 1592–1635 Nancy
Study of a Rearing Horse c. 1616

FIG 7 Antonio Tempesta, *Polonia oriundus*, British Museum, London

FIG 8 Jacques Callot, *Rearing Horse*, Albertina, Vienna

Brush and brown wash with
graphite, 16.7 × 14.1 cm
PURCHASED 1965
NO. 14836
WATERMARK
Fleur-de-lis
PROVENANCE
Geneviève Aymonier, Paris.

Although this sheet was long recognized as one of the many studies by Jacques
Callot after the *Cavalli di differenti paesi* series engraved by Tempesta in 1590,
Ternois reattributed it to an unknown hand.[1] Goldfarb had earlier noted similarities between the Ottawa drawing and the Tempesta print entitled *Polonia oriundus*
(fig. 7),[2] which was likely the source for a sheet held in the Albertina (fig. 8).[3] Callot's
horse studies date to his time in Florence (1615–17), where he developed a repertoire of models for use in battle scenes or equestrian portraits.[4] Lacking the backdrop landscapes of Tempesta and generally larger than his etchings, these studies
feature strong outlines and practically no modelling. Each sheet is drawn with sure,
swift strokes, often on both sides.

The Ottawa drawing differs in several respects from the studies after Tempesta.
Unlike Callot's subjects, the horse pictured here wears a harness and a saddle.
Essentially the product of brushwork, the sheet is painterly in nature, combining
dynamism and monumentality. Moreover, the iron gall ink (originally deep black,
now reddish-brown due to oxidation) was heightened with graphite for what must
have been an even more striking effect. The skilled hand that drew this equestrian
motif is clearly responsible as well for the freehand but absolutely unwavering
parallel lines, similar to burin marks, on the verso.

4

DANIEL DUMONSTIER
Paris 1574–1645 Paris

Portrait of an Ecclesiastic Wearing a Scarlet Biretta c. 1630

Black, red, and ochre chalks with
stump, laid down, 31.4 × 35.4 cm
PURCHASED 1956
NO. 6555
PROVENANCE
Colnaghi, London.

Some theories hold that this portrait represents Richelieu in 1622, shortly after he was ordained a cardinal. Popham's thesis is based on a comparison of a drawing attributed to Dumonstier and an engraved portrait by Lasne, purportedly of Richelieu, showing the features of a much older man.[1] The present author shares Goldfarb's reservations about the Lasne portrait.[2] Several young cardinals visited Paris during the 1620s, among them Louis Nogaret de La Valette-Épernon and Francesco Barberini, nephew of Pope Urban VIII, who is known to have stopped at Dumonstier's studio in 1625.[3] As well, there exist portraits after Dumonstier of another cardinal, Nicolas Coeffeteau, one engraved by Lasne in 1621 and the other by Mellan in 1623.[4] No likeness of these prelates presents an evident connection with the Ottawa drawing. On the other hand, Claude Mellan's 1636 engraved portrait of Richelieu's brother Alphonse de Richelieu, Cardinal of Lyons, bears a noticeable resemblance to the Ottawa subject.[5] In addition to the biretta and the pointed beard, it shows the same aquiline nose and long curly hair. The man in the engraving appears somewhat older than the one in the drawing, which probably was executed in 1630 following the elevation of Alphonse de Richelieu to the rank of cardinal. Although according to the information presented by Goldfarb,[6] Gilles Chomer dismisses this possibility.

While some aspects of the portrait may appear unfinished – the sketchily suggested garment, the crudely rendered biretta – Dumonstier has managed to lend the sitter an air of lively intelligence. It was no doubt these qualities that prompted Mariette to comment in his *Abecedario* that "one must not seek clever touches here, nor art nor colour, but accuracy and truth."[7] Dumonstier's "drawn" portraiture recalls that of Quesnel, Clouet, and others of their generation, but he had no qualms about embellishing his sitters, most of whom were members of court and high society with a keen appreciation for the prolific and colourful portraitist's wit. His contemporaries described him as a well-read and curious courtier in whose drawing room one met only the best people.[8] Many of his portraits, now dispersed in famous private and public collections, were copied by the greatest engravers of the day, including Crispin de Passe, Claude Mellan, Michel Lasne, and Abraham Bosse.[9]

5

Nicolas Lagneau
active c. 1600–1650
Portrait of an Old Woman n.d.

Black and red chalks, 34 × 24.1 cm
PURCHASED 1955
NO. 6560
PROVENANCE
K.E. Maison, London.

The attribution of this portrait of an old woman to Lagneau is based primarily on stylistic comparisons, though it is not always easy to find consistency among all the drawings ascribed to him. Here the subject was first captured in broad strokes of black and red chalk, then the modelling was rendered with a stump. The old woman, wearing a turban, is depicted bust-length and in three-quarters view, and she turns her wrinkled face towards us, showing a toothless smile. The Ottawa portrait can be compared to sheets held in the Louvre featuring likenesses of old women.[1] The "Lagneau Album" (Cabinet des estampes at the Bibliothèque nationale, Paris), so called by Jean Adhémar, contains other examples of the same genre.[2]

For the most part, the Lagneau corpus comprises "drawn portraits" of peasant-type characters with heavily emphasized features that at times verge on caricature. The artist's interest, it seems, lay more in reproducing types than in depicting individuals. This distinguishes his work from the court portraiture of Dumonstier, whose attention to detail makes it possible to identify some of the subjects. Theories vary as to the purpose of these sheets – physiognomic catalogues, characters drawn from the theatrical repertory, illustrations of "bizarre" faces[3] – but the fact that so many have survived, some in album form, implies that the genre was highly popular at the time.

The career span and precise identity of this enigmatic artist are still unclear.[4] Lagneau worked in the first half of the seventeenth century, but his somewhat archaistic style recalls that of the sixteenth-century draughtsmen who developed the portrait drawing genre, which remained in vogue into the late 1600s. With respect to manner and subject matter, Lagneau's drawings are reminiscent of Northern European art, or even of the Lorraine school.[5]

6

CLAUDE GELLÉE, CALLED LORRAIN

Chamagne 1604–1682 Rome

Landscape with Trees, Figures, and Cattle c. 1650

Pen and brown ink, 18.8 × 26.8 cm

PURCHASED 1971

NO. 16720

PROVENANCE

R. Davis; Colnaghi, London,
December 1935, no. 23 in sale
catalogue; H.S. Reitlinger, London;
Slatkin Gallery, New York, 1957–59;
Phyllis Lambert, New York;
Charles E. Slatkin, New York.

Opinions vary about the exact date of this drawing by Claude Gellée (known as Claude Lorrain), but it was probably done between the late 1640s and the early 1660s.[1] Initially, Roethlisberger connected it to two sheets from the *Liber Veritatis* (nos. 121 and 118)[2]: in the first, trees with the same foliage and positioning, as well as the shepherds in the foreground, demonstrate a composition similar to the Ottawa drawing; while in the second, the same graphic treatment is used to distinguish the different perspective planes. Russell established stylistic links with two much later sheets from the same album (nos. 147 and 149), stressing that drawings made solely with pen and ink – in contrast to more youthful efforts in wash – are characteristic of Lorrain's mature years, when he emphasized composition and the use of specific motifs. Note that this drawing was once thought to be related to the etching *The Wooden Bridge*, a debatable opinion now that Mannocci has dated that print to about 1638–41.[3]

The theme of shepherds leading or guarding their flocks recurs frequently in Lorrain's graphic works. Depicted in a bucolic setting, the cattle are usually a pretext for creating a certain harmony between successive dark and light planes. In the Ottawa example, the group at the extreme right of the sheet serves as a sort of *repoussoir* to draw the spectator into the scene.

7

CLAUDE GELLÉE, CALLED LORRAIN
Chamagne 1604–1682 Rome
Landscape with Saint John the Baptist Preaching 1655

Once more the artist takes up the subject of John the Baptist preaching, this time as recounted in Luke 3:1–18, where John proclaims the good news to the people. Despite the finished appearance of this sheet and the numerous studies on the same theme, Claude Lorrain produced no related paintings, as pointed out by Russell.[1] The John the Baptist theme recurs repeatedly in the artist's drawings. Roethlisberger more specifically identifies five drawings, including the one in Ottawa, that deal with John's preaching and date to 1655–56, in his view.[2] The inscription on the verso of the Ottawa sheet confirms this hypothesis. Of the five examples, the one held in Windsor Castle is closest in spirit to the Ottawa drawing, despite the inversion of values in the positioning of the background trees (fig. 9).[3]

A mature work of exceptional quality, the present drawing belongs to the stylistic period that historians term the "Grand Manner."[4] Beginning in the 1650s, Claude Lorrain "turned away from an emphasis on striking effects of light, preferring instead neutral or even daylight. Simultaneously he sought and achieved a more architectonically organized landscape, while the subject matter of his paintings was drawn increasingly from some of the most important or impressive episodes in sacred and profane literature."[5] He cultivated a passion for interpreting atmospheric phenomena in both his studies from nature and his compositional landscapes, drawing inspiration from the Roman campagna and Annibale Carracci's conception of the classical landscape.[6] The Ottawa sheet can also be linked to the painting on the same theme by Carracci, in Grenoble (fig. 10).[7]

Pen and brown ink, with brown
and grey wash, and graphite over
black chalk, heightened with
opaque white, on cream laid paper,
24.9 × 32.1 cm
PURCHASED 1940
NO. 4556
ANNOTATIONS
On the recto, lower right, towards
the centre, *17*; on the verso, along
the upper margin, in pen and
brown ink, *25*; at lower right, in pen
and brown ink, *1/12*; in graphite, *M*;
above the *M*, in graphite, *P*
INSCRIPTION
On the verso, bottom centre, in pen
and brown ink, *Claudi ... Gellee /
IV*[?]*] feci 1655 Roma*
PROVENANCE
P.H. Lankrink sale, 1693–94
(L. 2090); Richard Houlditch, died
1736 (L. 2214, followed by the
number *17* in pen and brown ink);
Viscountess Churchill; anonymous
sale, Sotheby's, London, 29 April
1937, no. 89; Colnaghi, London,
1937, no. 28 in sale catalogue.

FIG 9 Claude Gellée, called Lorrain,
Saint John the Baptist Preaching,
The Royal Collection, Her Majesty
Queen Elizabeth II

FIG 10 Annibale Carracci, *Sermon of Saint
John the Baptist*, Musée de Grenoble

8

Gaspard Dughet
Rome 1615–1675 Rome

Rocky Landscape c. 1665

Black chalk and graphite with
white chalk on blue paper,
21.2 × 37.4 cm
PURCHASED 1965
NO. 14690
PROVENANCE
Benjamin West; William, 7th Count
of Dartmouth; Colnaghi, London.

This rocky landscape is a preparatory drawing for the decorative program executed around 1667 that was commissioned by Lorenzo Onofrio Colonna for the family palace on the Piazza Santi Apostoli in Rome. It relates to a gouache *modello* for an overdoor (fig. 11).[1] As Boisclair notes, Gaspard Dughet's renown is due in large part to the Palazzo Colonna frescoes.[2] Four other black chalk drawings on blue paper dating to Dughet's early period of maturity are associated with the same cycle.[3] All of the drawings in this series are of similar composition and technique: the hardness of the rock is rendered with hatching or cross-hatching, while the chiaroscuro is obtained by alternating reserves and saturated black areas to extremely dramatic effect. The sky is reduced, leaving the stage to untamed nature. In its emphasis on jagged rock formations and illustration of a wild, steeply angled site, larger than life, this sheet recalls *A Rocky Landscape with Two Figures* by Salvator Rosa, in the Galleria Nazionale d'Arte Antica, Rome.[4]

Dughet was strongly influenced by Poussin, his brother-in-law, whose studio he joined at the age of fifteen. But his interpretation of landscape soon diverged from the master's classicism, focusing instead on nature as primitive, even hostile, and depicted in stark contrasts.[5] Rocks, waterfalls, and vegetation are shaped by vigorous lines in his drawings, with contrasting light and shade helping to create atmospheric effects. Although Dughet was influenced by Claude Lorrain in Rome, the spontaneity of his black chalk studies sets him apart.

FIG 11 Gaspard Dughet, *Rocky Landscape with a Natural Vault*, Galleria Colonna, Rome

9

Jean Cotelle I
Meaux 1607–1676 Paris
Design for a Ceiling Decoration c. 1660

Pen and brown ink with grey wash,
over traces of black and red chalks,
formerly laid down, 35.6 × 25.8 cm
PURCHASED 1938
NO. 4442
ANNOTATION
At upper right, on the mounting, 76
PROVENANCE
Pier Leone Ghezzi, 18th century;
H. Burg, London.

This sheet comes from an album that once belonged to the Roman artist Pier Leone Ghezzi, a caricaturist and collector of architectural drawings. It relates to the seventy-two drawings that make up the Ashmolean Museum album, some of which are attributed to Cotelle.[1] Numerous other drawings in this genre by Cotelle are found at the Swedish Nationalmuseum and at the Hermitage. Some of the sheets that illustrate ceilings (few of which have survived) were engraved by Jean Boulanger and François de Poilly and later gathered in a book dedicated to Anne de Rohan, *Livre De divers Ornements pour Plafonds, Cintres Surbaissez, Galleries et autres*, published around 1660.[2]

Popham was the first to ascribe the Ottawa example to Cotelle on the grounds of stylistic similarity with the Oxford drawings. The original owner remains unknown, although the monogram *CAV* at the centre right of the sheet suggests a commission by César, Duke of Vendôme, and Alexandre, Grand Prior of France, two brothers who lived at the Hôtel de Vendôme, which was demolished during the reign of Louis XIV to create what is now the Place Vendôme. The presence of a somewhat similar monogram in a drawing at the Ashmolean, carrying the number 66 on its mounting, has been scrutinized by scholars.[3] Their differing interpretations notwithstanding, the entwined letters surmounted by a crown could very well refer to César's ducal crown, as suggested by Cazort in 1970.[4]

After studying with Laurent Guyot and assisting in Vouet's studio, Jean Cotelle I designed Gobelin tapestries in 1633 before being named an ornamental painter to the king. Granted a royal pension in 1650, he was one of the first masters to become a member of the Académie royale de peinture et de sculpture. He owed his fame to ceiling designs, especially the decorations on mythological themes at the Hôtel de Rohan, the Tuileries, the Louvre, and Fontainebleau.

The 17th and 18th Centuries

The Academic Tradition

10

CHARLES LE BRUN
Paris 1619–1690 Paris

Study for "Fame" for an Allegorical Composition in Honour of Cardinal de Richelieu c. 1641–42

Black chalk, heightened with white chalk, 25.5 × 40.3 cm

PURCHASED 1955

NO. 6318

WATERMARK
Grapes, similar to Heawood 2100

PROVENANCE
H.M. Calmann, London.

Formerly attributed to Simon Vouet, this drawing bears eloquent witness to the training and early career of Charles Le Brun.[1] After a brief apprenticeship with François Perrier, the budding artist enjoyed the patronage of Chancellor Séguier, who introduced him to Simon Vouet. By the late 1630s, Le Brun was already demonstrating the benefits of the master's instruction, notably in the "thesis drawings" that he produced for doctoral students at Université de Paris. At the time, candidates used to publish their theses with an allegorical frontispiece dedicated to an eminent person.[2] *Study for "Fame"* confirms that the young man had already mastered the art of volumes learned from Vouet. Le Brun's ingenious use of space is also worthy of note: the figure is placed along the diagonal axis of the sheet, prefiguring its positioning in the later engraved composition.

Jennifer Montagu was the first to attribute this sheet to Le Brun in connection with the engraving by Michel Lasne,[3] *Allegorical Composition in Honour of Cardinal de Richelieu* (fig. 12), meant to adorn the thesis of Jean Ruzé d'Effiat, Abbot of Saint-Sernin in Toulouse, which was dedicated to the cardinal in 1642. The central portion, with the dedication, was never completed;[4] the same year, Richelieu had the doctoral candidate's brother, Henri Coëffier de Ruzé, Marquis of Cinq-Mars, executed for treason. A complex allegorical program designed to extol the Richelieu administration is evident nonetheless.[5] The Ottawa drawing is a preparatory study for the figure of Fame located in the upper-right corner of the print. Trumpeting Fame, her banner bearing the Latin inscription CRESCIT EVNDO ("It grows as it goes") is a counterpart to the Génie de la France (Spirit of France) figure presenting a globe adorned with fleurs-de-lis to the statesman. As was his custom, Le Brun made numerous studies for this composition.[6] The Metropolitan Museum of Art holds a preliminary drawing for the lower section representing Mars and Apollo (fig. 13),[7] and there is a detail for a caryatid at the Pierpont Morgan Library.[8]

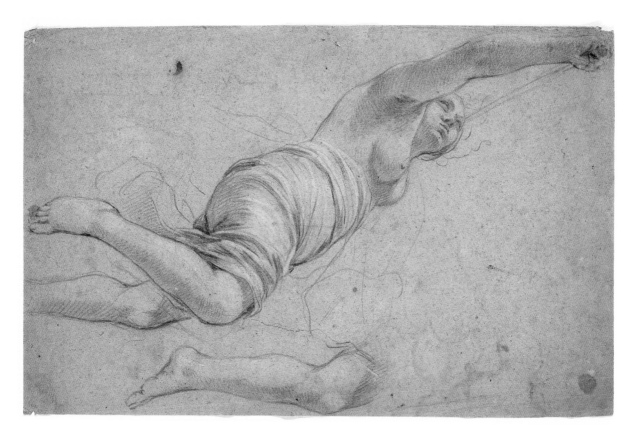

FIG 12 Michel Lasne, *Allegorical Composition in Honour of Cardinal de Richelieu*, Bibliothèque nationale, Paris

FIG 13 Charles Le Brun, *Allegory in Honour of Cardinal de Richelieu*, The Metropolitan Museum of Art, New York, Harry G. Sperling Fund, 1974

II
CHARLES DE LA FOSSE
Paris 1636–1716 Paris

Study of Nestor and His Associates, after Peter Paul Rubens c. 1670–79

FIG 14 Rubens, *The Wrath of Achilles*, Courtauld
Institute, London

FIG 15 Charles de La Fosse, *The Presentation of the
Virgin at the Temple*, Musée des Augustins, Toulouse

Red and black chalks heightened
with white on light brown laid
paper, 47.5 × 27.1 cm
PURCHASED 2001
NO. 40610
ANNOTATION
At lower right, in brown ink, *Paul
Rubbens*
PROVENANCE
Antenor Patino collection; Michel
Gierzod, Paris.

This previously unpublished study[1] in three chalks reproduces a detail from Rubens' *The Wrath of Achilles*, c. 1630–35, one of eight scenes designed to illustrate the life of Achilles in tapestry form. For this drawing, Charles de La Fosse copied the *modello*, which is now in the Courtauld Institute (fig. 14). Achilles' wrath is aroused when Agamemnon lays claim to his slave Briseis, but the goddess Athena intervenes to prevent him from raising his sword. At the left, Diomedes and old Nestor move forward in an attempt to calm the antagonists. Although it is not known in what circumstances La Fosse could have seen the *modello*,[2] his drawings after Rubens date to the 1670s.[3] His fondness for the work of the Flemish master and for the three-coloured chalk drawing technique led him to join the colourist faction at the Académie, where he was appointed director in 1699.

In all likelihood, this clear, precise studio drawing later served as a model for one of La Fosse's greatest works, *The Presentation of the Virgin at the Temple* (fig. 15),[4] painted in 1682 for the Notre-Dame du Mont-Carmel chapel at the Carmelite convent in Toulouse. In the foreground of the painting, now in the Musée des Augustins in Toulouse, the pose of Joachim, Mary's father, recalls the Ottawa drawing. The expressions of the two protagonists are markedly different, but their postures are similar. In each case, the old man is climbing a stair, his body bent slightly forwards and his amply draped garment revealing the influence of Rubens. The presence of this draping in *The Presentation* closely echoes Rubens' mature work, while once again demonstrating La Fosse's penchant for the Baroque.[5] Several drawings for *The Presentation* are known, including a head study for the Virgin at the Metropolitan Museum of Art (fig. 16).[6] A compositional drawing at the Nationalmuseum in Stockholm presents the composition of the painting in reverse and is rendered differently, with heavily drawn outlines.[7]

FIG 16 Charles de La Fosse, *Head of a Young Girl and Studies of Her Hands and Right Foot*, The Metropolitan Museum of Art, New York, Harry G. Sperling Fund, 1980

12
Raymond de La Fage
Lisle-sur-Tarn 1656–1684 Lyons
Ecce Homo c. 1682

Pen and brown ink, grey and
greenish-ochre wash, laid down on
wove paper, 18.5 × 14.4 cm
PURCHASED 1911
NO. 282
PROVENANCE
Duke of Rutland; Gimpel and
Wildenstein, New York.

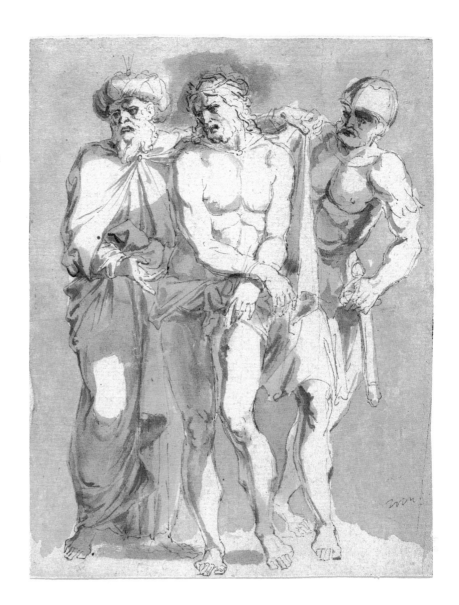

FIG 17 After Rubens, *Ecce Homo*, Gabinetto Nazionale delle Stampe, Rome

FIG 18 Raymond de La Fage, *Ecce Homo*, Christ Church Museum, Oxford

All evidence indicates that this *Ecce Homo* is after a Flemish engraving by an unknown seventeenth-century artist (fig. 17) inspired by Rubens' *Christ before Pilate*.[1] The three-figure composition is unusual in the work of Raymond de La Fage, who typically favoured crowd scenes overflowing with action. Although Christ's pose differs from the engraving, he is still flanked by a Roman soldier and a Jew, identified by his turban. There is a larger and more finished version of this scene, with incision marks, at the Christ Church Museum in Oxford (fig. 18).[2] Notable on the Oxford sheet are the different stance of the Roman soldier, the addition of a reed in Christ's hand, and, especially, the architectural backdrop suggested by broad ruled lines that contrast with the fluid, rippling lines of the bodies. The finished appearance of this sheet and its incised outlines suggest that it was intended for engraving. The Ottawa drawing, similar in several respects to a sheet sold at Christie's in 1958 and mentioned by Popham,[3] can thus be considered an earlier work, or perhaps a preliminary sketch.

La Fage's hand is recognizable in the spontaneity of his pen and blackish-brown ink compositions, occasionally heightened with grey wash. In Rome, his depictions of muscular bodies in exaggerated poses earned him a reputation as a new Michelangelo. And although he drew religious, mythological, and battle scenes, his bacchanalia branded him as a non-conformist artist, leading a life of debauchery. He died at the early age of twenty-eight, but left a substantial corpus of drawings that Mariette lauded in his *Abecedario*.[4] A meeting between La Fage and the Flemish engraver and publisher Jan Van der Bruggen in 1682 resulted in the posthumous publication of the French artist's drawings.

13

JEAN-BAPTISTE CORNEILLE
Paris 1649–1695 Paris
Moses and the Burning Bush c. 1690–95

Pen and dark brown ink with grey wash and black chalk, 12.6 × 14.9 cm (irreg.)
PURCHASED with funds provided by the Friends of the Print Room Trust, 2002
NO. 40965
PROVENANCE
Lutz Riester, Freiburg im Breisgau, Germany.

This ink-and-wash drawing illustrates a scene from the Old Testament story of Moses and the Burning Bush (Exodus 3:1–4). While Moses was grazing his flock at Horeb, the mountain of God, God appeared to him in the midst of a bush that blazed but was not consumed. Jean-Baptiste Corneille pictures Moses at the left of the image, with his flock in the background, while God and an angel are visible in a thick cloud at the upper right. Writhing at Moses' feet is his shepherd's crook transformed into a serpent, symbol of the "miraculous power granted by Yahweh to Aaron and Moses to impress the Pharaoh" when demanding the release of the Jews.[1]

Despite its small size, *Moses and the Burning Bush* is easily compared to a drawing in the Ashmolean Museum, *The Fall of the Giants* (fig. 19),[2] in terms of vigorous composition and nervous pen strokes. The same staging determined by the opposition of heavenly powers and earthly beings is found in Corneille's *Jupiter Casting Vulcan from Mount Olympus*. But while this painting relates more closely to the Ashmolean drawing,[3] the layout and iconography of the Ottawa sheet recall the painting on the same theme executed by Nicolas Poussin for Cardinal de Richelieu in 1641 (fig. 20).[4]

Corneille's personality is no doubt most manifest in his drawings, where his flamboyant style is expressed in vibrant, spontaneous pen work and dramatically staged scenes that often radiate an aura of strangeness. Most of his surviving works date to between 1690 and 1695 and reveal a singular artist whose oeuvre attests a certain filiation with the Baroque in "the dynamism of his compositions, the overstated gestures and expressions of his characters, the flowing draperies."[5] It may be that this tendency is related to the Rubéniste influence found in the theories of Roger de Piles, for whom Corneille engraved the figures for *Premiers éléments de la peinture pratique* (1684).

FIG 19 Jean-Baptiste Corneille, *The Fall of the Giants*, Ashmolean Museum, Oxford

FIG 20 Nicolas Poussin, *Moses and the Burning Bush*, Statens Museum for Kunst, Copenhagen

14

ANTOINE COYPEL
Paris 1661–1722 Paris

A Faun Seated on a Balustrade c. 1695

Black and red chalks, heightened
with white chalk on brown laid
paper, 38 × 27.3 cm
PURCHASED 1956
NO. 6827
PROVENANCE
Colnaghi, London, no. 43 in sale
catalogue.

FIG 22 Annibale Carracci, *Seated Ignudo for the Farnese Gallery*, Musée des Beaux-Arts et d'Archéologie, Besançon

FIG 21 Antoine Coypel, *A Seated Faun*, Ashmolean Museum, Oxford

Formerly attributed to Louis de Boullogne on the basis of its association with an album of drawings that included academic nudes dated and signed by him,[1] this study of a faun is now ascribed by some scholars to Antoine Coypel.[2] The album also included other sheets by Coypel on the same theme, all executed *aux trois crayons* and exhibiting the same formal characteristics. Among these, Popham notes a *Seated Faun* study (fig. 21).[3] Despite their similarities, none of these sheets relates to a particular project, as Jon Whiteley points out.

In contrast, the Ottawa study bears an appreciable resemblance to one of the *ignudi* that adorn the upper corners of the frames at the Farnese Gallery in Rome, for which the Musée de Besançon has a study by Annibale Carracci (fig. 22).[4] Created between 1597 and 1600, Carracci's decorative cycle exerted a major influence on the development of French art. Charles Errard, the first director of the Académie de France in Rome, commissioned young artists to copy the entire work for the purpose of embellishing the Galerie des Ambassadeurs at the Tuileries, where decoration began in 1670. Engravings by Jacques Belly from 1641 and Carlo Cesi from 1657, after Annibale Carracci, doubtless served as models for Coypel's contemporaries as well, as did some of the original drawings by the Bolognese master that belonged to the Jabach Collection and later to the Royal Collection. Certain studies in the manner of Carracci now in the Louvre and ascribed to Le Brun or to the Boullogne brothers (Louis in particular) recall the extraordinary influence of the Bolognese model. The fluid lines, distinct contours, and precisely rendered modelling seen in most of these cases lead to the conclusion that the Louvre drawings and the Ottawa drawing share a common model.[5]

15

ANTOINE COYPEL
Paris 1661–1722 Paris

Torso of a Female Nude: Study for "The Triumph of Venus" c. 1698–1700

Red chalk and pale pink opaque
bodycolour with touches of
graphite, squared with red chalk for
transfer, on grey paper,
41.8 × 51.6 cm
PURCHASED 1983
NO. 28313
PROVENANCE
Pamela Gordon, Paris.

Squared and traced in red chalk on the verso, this smoothly rendered study was drawn in preparation for the painting *Venus in a Conch Shell Carried by Three Tritons* (fig. 23), made around 1700 for the Ménagerie at Versailles.[1] The decorative program for the little château was guided by the tastes of the king, who desired "that youthfulness be incorporated into whatever is done."[2] In other words, the sovereign's aesthetic leanings favoured gallant mythology over the Grand Manner prescribed by the Académie.

With slight variations, drawings, paintings, and prints testify to the importance, at various times in Coypel's career, of the "goddess with outstretched arms" motif. One example that springs to mind is *Venus Frolicking in the Sea with Nymphs and Putti,* executed for the future Regent around 1700–02.[3] An engraving by D. Beauvais (Nicolas-Dauphin de Beauvais) reflects the painting that adorned the main vault of the royal palace gallery, *Aeneas's Ships Changed into Nymphs,* 1703–06, in which the arms and head of the Aeneas figure are in the same position as in the Ottawa drawing.[4]

Originally trained in the strict classical tradition by his father, Noël Coypel, Antoine soon joined Charles de La Fosse, Jean Jouvenet, the Boullogne brothers, and the other colourists at the Académie. During the 1690s, as Garnier notes, a dearth of royal commissions pushed him to seek private patrons.[5] From then on, he adopted an airy, even gracious style designed to please a clientele partial to light-spirited paintings, paving the way for the Rococo vogue that would flourish early in the next century. However, the lessons learned from Raphael, the Carraccis, and Domenichino, as well as from Correggio's grand decorative ensembles were not forgotten, and late in his career he returned to classicism in the history painting tradition.

FIG 23 Antoine Coypel, *Venus in a Conch Shell Carried by Three Tritons*, Musée du Louvre, Département des peintures, Paris

16
PIERRE-JACQUES CAZES
Paris 1676–1754 Paris
The Consecration of Saint Augustine c. 1702

Black chalk and grey wash,
heightened with opaque white on
blue laid paper, 40 × 26.4 cm
PURCHASED 1983
NO. 28189
WATERMARK
Heawood 3020 (Amsterdam 1702)
PROVENANCE
Christopher Comer, Paris; Cythera
Fine Arts Inc., St. Albans, Vermont.

FIG 24 Louis de Boullogne,
The Consecration of Saint Augustine,
Musée du Louvre, Cabinet des
dessins, Paris

FIG 25 Louis de Boullogne,
The Consecration of Saint Augustine,
Musée des Beaux-Arts, Dijon

Attributed to Louis de Boullogne the Younger when it was acquired, this sheet must instead be considered the work of Pierre-Jacques Cazes by reason of its stylistic effects, in the opinion of Jean-François Méjanès.[1] This artist's same technique can be seen in a drawing in the Musée de Beaux-Arts de Rennes, *The Martyrdom of Saint Lawrence.* In both examples, the figures and scenery are first laid in delicately in black chalk. Grey wash is then broadly applied to simulate areas in shadow; the figures in the foreground are emphasized with opaque white, while intermediate planes are highlighted with a lighter touch.

This drawing, which according to the watermark dates to after 1702, has some connection with the most important royal commission of the era, the decoration of the Église du Dôme at Hôtel des Invalides in Paris, which was carried out primarily between 1702 and 1704.[2] Of the four chapels dedicated to the Church Fathers, the one entrusted to Louis de Boullogne was the Chapel of Saint Augustine; his preliminary drawings for the six frescoes depicting the principal episodes in the life of the saint are today in the Louvre. We can observe that the study by Boullogne for the *Consecration of Saint Augustine* (fig. 24) has little to do with the Ottawa drawing described above, despite comparable dimensions and the use of blue paper in both cases.[3] Boullogne sketched his composition as a tangle of lines in black and white chalks, and the completed work, as seen in an engraving by Charles-Nicolas Cochin[4] and in a replica in Dijon (fig. 25), also departs significantly from the work attributed to Cazes. Among the main differences, the Boullogne version of the scene shows the saint already wearing a mitre and accompanied by a bishop, and the figure of the cardinal in the left foreground serves as a *repoussoir.* A series of ten pictures also exists, which were intended for the refectory of the monastery of the Barefoot Augustines in the Place des Victoires and can be dated to the same period as the execution of the decoration of Les Invalides.[5] The six themes used in the Chapel of Saint Augustine, including the *Consecration of Saint Augustine* in a painting by Hilaire Olivet, are treated in quite another manner; the horizontal format of the Olivet painting and the difference in spirit of its composition discourage the assumption that it bears a relation to the Ottawa drawing.

Nothing indicates that Cazes took an active part in decorating the interior of the corner chapel in Les Invalides, but we do know that he was one of the many students of Louis de Boullogne and his elder brother Bon.[6] Cazes won the Prix de Rome in 1699 before being accepted to the Académie in 1703, but did not make the journey to Italy because of a lack of funds.[7] It is perhaps a reasonable conjecture that Cazes was called upon at that time to participate in the major decoration project under the supervision of, or even in competition with, one of his mentors.

17
PIERRE-JACQUES CAZES
Paris 1676–1754 Paris
Hercules and the Tunic of Nessus after 1728

This drawing recounts the final moments of the life of Hercules, the most celebrated hero of classical mythology. Sentenced to twelve labours for murders committed while in a fit of madness, he now submits to the ultimate punishment of donning a tunic poisoned by his wife, Deianeira. Unwittingly, she had soaked it not in a love potion, but in the deadly blood of the centaur Nessus, Hercules' enemy. The scene shows Hercules in the foreground, wild with pain and struggling to free himself from the excruciating tunic, while a divinity – Athena? – tries to restrain him. His attributes, the lion's skin and serpent, are depicted at his feet. At the lower right lies Lichas, the companion who brought him the garment, who was grabbed by the foot and hurled into the sea by the frenzied Hercules.[1]

The attribution of the drawing to Pierre-Jacques Cazes has been confirmed by Pierre Rosenberg.[2] *Hercules and the Tunic of Nessus* has the formal characteristics typical of this artist's drawings: generous use of wash, and figures with elongated bodies and fixed expressions, in well-balanced compositions. The squaring suggests that the sheet was transferred to another format or technique, an engraving or a painting. The date corresponding to the watermark – 1728 – supports the theory that *Hercules* was made while Cazes was teaching at the Académie.

Although admired by his contemporaries, Cazes' graphic oeuvre appears to have fallen out of favour until the publication of an article by Pierre Rosenberg and Isabelle Julia listing some eighty pieces.[3] Best known as a painter of commissions for religious congregations,[4] Caze executed works with historical, mythological, and allegorical themes as well. He also produced drawings that were used to illustrate books and historical series.

Pen and grey ink, brush with grey
wash, squared with black chalk for
transfer, 24.6 × 34.6 cm

PURCHASED 2003

NO. 41190

WATERMARK

Heawood 2282 (France, 1728)

PROVENANCE

Lutz Riester, Freiburg im Breisgau,
Germany.

18
CHARLES PARROCEL
Paris 1688–1752 Paris
Battle Scene n.d.

Red chalk, 32.5 × 52.2 cm
Gift of Theodore Allen Heinrich,
1978
NO. 18969
INSCRIPTION
At lower right, in brown ink,
Parrocel 171[6]

FIG 26 Antonio Tempesta, *Illustration for Canto IX, from*
"Jerusalem Delivered II," British Museum, London

This highly intense composition in red chalk includes elements inspired by a scene from the series engraved by Antonio Tempesta (fig. 26) after the verse epic *Jerusalem Delivered* by Torquato Tasso.[1] In both cases, mounted soldiers in classical helmets and Turks recognizable by their turbans clash in a tumult of men and horses. With fluid, spirited lines, Charles Parrocel creates a sense of surging movement by making the distant Turkish horde converge towards the mêlée in the right foreground. The group of three figures in the upper area – apparently infidels torturing a proselyte – is no doubt an allusion to the spirit of the Crusades. In spite of shadows rendered by summary hatching and an occasionally hasty hand, Parrocel's style is efficient and was much admired in his day.[2]

The date inscribed on the sheet, although incomplete, would suggest that the work was executed during the artist's time at the Académie de France in Rome – 1713 to 1716 – where *turqueries* were very popular with the students.[3] This vogue of exoticism no doubt stemmed from the Austrian-Ottoman wars that raged early in the century; as Sophie Raux notes, Parrocel repeatedly depicted scenes of battle between European and Turkish troops.[4] Turkish soldiers, in particular, are the subject of many of his studies now in collections in Lyons, Orléans, and Lille.[5] Mariette mentions that Parrocel was commissioned to portray the arrival of the Turkish ambassador in Paris in 1723.[6]

One sheet in the Musée de Lille featuring horsemen charging at a gallop, with a church in the background (fig. 27), exhibits the same graphic verve as the red chalk Ottawa drawing. The date written on the Lille drawing, 1750, indicates that the work was executed two years before the artist's death. The date on the Ottawa sheet, *171*[6], while corresponding to Parrocel's early career, may actually be an allusion to the conflict between Turks and Austrians at that time. As Hélène Rihal points out, the context in which this drawing was done remains vague; Parrocel appears to have produced a great many drawings for the sole purpose of creating a catalogue of models for his paintings.[7] In any case, decades after its conclusion, this war again fired the imagination of the artist, who here combines a specific historical backdrop and a battle scene tradition handed down by Joseph Parrocel, his father.

FIG 27 Charles Parrocel, *Horsemen Charging at a Gallop*, Musée des Beaux-Arts, Lille

19

FRANÇOIS BOUCHER
Paris 1703–1770 Paris
Preparatory Study for "The Judgement of Susannah" c. 1722

Red chalk with touches of black
chalk, 24 × 32.4 cm
PURCHASED 1997
NO. 38550
PROVENANCE
Sale, Sotheby's, London, 2 July
1997, lot 65.

This preliminary drawing by François Boucher is to date the only known composition study for *The Judgement of Susannah* (fig. 28), the painting that marked the beginning of the artist's career before he began studying with François Lemoyne. In his exhaustive analysis of the painting, which is still dated only approximately, Colin B. Bailey traces its sources meticulously.[1] The subject, rarely used in French painting, is taken from an Old Testament text (Daniel 13:28–59) that recounts young Daniel's intervention to save Susannah from certain death after two old men have accused her of adultery. It is likely that Boucher was inspired by the Book of Daniel in a version of the Holy Bible published by Le Maistre de Saci in 1717; moreover, passages in a poem that appeared in 1722 in the *Mercure de France* praised the painting *Susannah Accused by the Elders* by Antoine Coypel, a few months after that artist's death, and the young Boucher may well have interpreted this as a challenge.

The drawing differs markedly from the painting, but the setting and the position of the groups of figures foreshadow the final work. In the preparatory drawing, with its nervous line, accents in black chalk around the figure of Daniel make him the central point of the composition. Boucher's beginnings remain enigmatic despite the fact that a number of scholars have investigated the subject.[2] Bailey has nonetheless identified a stylistic kinship with the sheets in the series drawn for the *History of France*, which represent a definite point of departure for situating this drawing and the painting. Executed mainly with pen and wash in about 1727, these preliminary drawings demonstrate a similar format, the same verve in their composition, and a common source of inspiration for the setting.[3]

Among the holdings of the National Gallery of Canada is the drawing of a detail related to the painting, but its timid, overly careful rendering leads us to attribute it to a hand other than Boucher's. The drawn fragment (fig. 29) repeats a section at the extreme left of the painting, which differs only in the presence of a sphinx instead of a lion, leading Alastair Laing to put forward the idea that the drawing is evidence of a subsequent modification by Boucher.[4]

FIG 28 François Boucher, *The Judgement of Susannah*, NGC

FIG 29 After François Boucher, *Detail from "The Judgement of Susannah,"* NGC

20

FRANÇOIS BOUCHER

Paris 1703–1770 Paris

An Angel Bringing Food to a Hermit n.d.

Black chalk, 31.6 × 21.6 cm
Gift of Mrs. Samuel Bronfman,
Montreal, 1957
NO. 6888

PROVENANCE
Blind stamp, at lower right, G
(L. 1119); private collection, London;[1]
Charles E. Slatkin, New York;
Mrs. Samuel Bronfman, Montreal.

FIG 30 Simone Cantarini, *An Angel
Appearing to Saint Joseph*, Städelsches
Kunstinstitut, Frankfurt

The theme of this drawing — an angel feeding a hermit — could conceivably refer to an incident in the Old Testament where Elijah is fed by an angel (1 Kings 19:5–8). But the composition surely draws in part on an engraving by Jan Saenredam after Bloemaert, *Elijah Fed by Two Ravens*.[2] François Boucher's early interest in the work of Abraham Bloemaert took concrete form in 1735 with the publication of his *Studies*, a collection of pastoral and rustic scenes after the Flemish master.[3]

Stylistically, this black chalk drawing rendered in lines more allusive than descriptive recalls the decisive influence of certain High Baroque Italian masters on the young Boucher.[4] The composition presents strong similarities to a study by Simone Cantarini for *An Angel Appearing to Saint Joseph* (fig. 30). Of particular note is the position of the angel, which in both drawings creates the same diagonal, proceeding from the shoulder along the outstretched arm.

It is difficult to date this sheet, which served as a model for Fragonard's first etching, executed between 1752 and 1756 while he attended Boucher's studio (fig. 31).[5] The composition may equally well date to Boucher's stay in Italy, between 1728 and 1730, which would account for its formal relationship to a drawing and a painting by Pierre-Charles Trémolières, *Hagar and the Angel* (fig. 32).[6] Furthermore, Brugerolles establishes a parallel between the Trémolières work and a painting by Boucher, *Hagar and Ishmael in the Desert*, c. 1735, whose similar composition and iconography reveal Trémolières' influence on Boucher, if not a common source of inspiration.[7] Nevertheless, as several scholars have noted, the chronology of Boucher's works remains complicated by his eclectic training — influenced by a variety of movements — and his propensity to revisit certain themes throughout his career, as seems to be the case here.[8]

FIG 31 Jean-Honoré Fragonard, *A Hermit Saint in the Desert*, NGC

FIG 32 Pierre-Charles Trémolières, *Hagar and the Angel*, École nationale supérieure des beaux-arts, Paris

21
MICHEL-FRANÇOIS DANDRÉ-BARDON
Aix-en-Provence 1700–1783 Paris

Apollo and the Muses with Parnassus in the Middle Distance: Study for the Painted Decoration of a Concert Hall in the Town Hall of Aix-en-Provence c. 1740

Pen and brown ink with brown
wash on black chalk, 15.4 × 37.3 cm
PURCHASED 1952
NO. 6047
PROVENANCE
Colnaghi, London, no. 24 in
sale catalogue.

This sheet, like the one in the Ashmolean which is almost identical to it (fig. 33), was long attributed to the Venetian artist G.B. Crosato, until Pierre Rosenberg identified its subject in 1972.

In 1740, Michel-François Dandré-Bardon painted a decorative work for a new musical society that had had a hall donated to it on the ground floor of the town hall of Aix-en-Provence. The artist's biographer, Claude-Jacques-Henri d'Ageville, describes the work as a trompe-l'oeil painting that covered the back wall and created an illusion that made the hall where musicians and spectators gathered seem larger.[1] The Goncourts described another drawing related to the same project, at one time in their collection, which showed "Apollo, one hand propped on his lyre and surrounded by the Muses, in a room bounded by a balustrade, with Cupids hanging draperies on its columns."[2] Similar in several aspects to the first two, this slightly larger study is currently in the Horvitz collection.

In the Ottawa drawing, the outline of Mount Parnassus can be glimpsed in the background, while the scene is bounded on the left by a musician holding a viol and on the right by a parliamentarian displaying a document. Rosenberg has connected it with Dandré-Bardon's *Councillor in the Parliament of Aix-en-Provence*, 1733, in the Royal Museum of Fine Arts, Antwerp.[3] Note that this variation on the same theme illustrates the artist's habit of repeating his allegorical compositions.[4]

Apollo and the Muses shows some of the distinctive characteristics of Dandré-Bardon's pen-and-ink drawings: a fine, nervous line with an almost telegraphic rendering, generous use of wash, and elaborate composition. Thus it is possible to concur with Rosenberg and Chol, who have detected in Dandré-Bardon's work the influence of Venetian artists such as Piazzetta and Tiepolo who were his contemporaries.[5]

FIG 33 Michel-François Dandré-Bardon, *Study for a Mural with Apollo and the Muses*, Ashmolean Museum, Oxford

22
CHARLES-JOSEPH NATOIRE
Nîmes 1700–1777 Castel Gandolfo
The Marriage of Alexander and Roxane c. 1757

FIG 34 Charles Natoire, *The Conclusion of the Peace of Taranto*, Musée des Beaux-Arts, Nîmes

FIG 35 Studio of Raphael, *The Marriage of Alexander and Roxane*, Borghese Gallery, Rome

Pen and brown ink with brown
wash, heightened with opaque
white over black chalk and
graphite, on blue laid paper, laid
down, 32.5 × 41.1 cm
PURCHASED 1976
NO. 18658
INSCRIPTION
At lower right, *C NATOIRE*
PROVENANCE
J. Formingé collection, Paris;
H. Shickman Gallery, New York.

FIG 36 Charles-Nicolas Cochin the
Elder, *The Marriage of Alexander and
Roxane*, Bibliothèque nationale, Paris

FIG 37 Tommaso (di Andrea)
Vincidor, *Hymen, Cupid, and
Alexander Offering the Crown to Roxane*,
Musée du Louvre, Cabinet des
dessins, Paris

Susanna Caviglia-Brunel believes that this drawing by Charles-Joseph Natoire was executed around 1757, on the basis of the technical and stylistic affinities between it and his studies for the series of seven paintings intended to illustrate *The History of Mark Antony and Cleopatra* (1753–57).[1] We refer more specifically to a sketch in Nîmes, *The Conclusion of the Peace of Taranto* (fig. 34), painted for that series. In the Nîmes composition, Augustus, at the centre, resembles in his placement and costume the figure of Alexander in the Ottawa drawing.[2] According to Duclaux, drawings done in brown wash, such as *The Marriage of Alexander and Roxane*, demonstrate the sort of pictorial experimentation at the technical level that Natoire pursued, particularly after his arrival in Rome in 1751.[3]

Natoire's interpretation of *The Marriage of Alexander and Roxane* derives from a long iconographic tradition whose origin goes back to the Hellenic era, specifically to a painting by Aetion. Since the Renaissance, a number of artists had been inspired by the poet Lucian's description of it (*Herodotus Sive Aetion*, 4–6): seated on the marriage bed, the modest Roxane is represented with downcast eyes, while one Cupid removes her veil and another takes off her shoes. Standing before her, Alexander the Great offers her a crown; he is accompanied by his friend Hephaistos, who carries a burning torch, and by Hymen, god of marriage. Two drawings by Raphael illustrating the episode, one a pen-and-ink sketch in the Teyler Museum, Haarlem,[4] and the other, a more elaborate composition in pen and wash with white highlights (location unknown), became reference points for subsequent versions. The composition by Raphael inspired a fresco at the Olgiati-Bevilacqua casino (fig. 35), attributed to Siciolante da Sermoneta, as well as another painted circa 1516–17 by Sodoma, in the Villa Farnesine, Rome. Around 1559–60, Taddeo Zuccaro also executed a fresco at the Palazzo Mattei (now Caetani), for which a pen-and-wash drawing exists.[5] In France, around 1541–44, le Primatrice painted the marriage of Alexander and Roxane for the bedroom of the Duchesse d'Étampes in the Château de Fontainebleau.[6]

For the drawing in Ottawa, Natoire used as his model a print that Charles-Nicolas Cochin the Elder engraved in 1729 (fig. 36) after the more successful of the compositions by Raphael,[7] which had itself been engraved by Jacopo Caraglio. The Raphael drawing seems to have inspired many copies, including one by the Bolognese Tommaso Vincidor (fig. 37).[8] Between 1684 and 1686, the sheet by this collaborator of Raphael, which entered the collection of the king in 1671, served as a model for Antoine Coypel when he was creating a cartoon for a tapestry after drawings attributed to Raphael,[9] as part of a royal commission.

23
Jean-Honoré Fragonard
Grasse 1732–1806 Paris
Medea Slaying Her Children c. 1761

Black chalk, mounted on laid
paper, 21.1 × 24.8 cm
Gift of the Royal Trust Company,
Montreal, 1962
NO. 9843
PROVENANCE
Collection Philippe Gille, 1888;
Madame Gille; anonymous sale, 21
March 1956, no. 11; Charles E.
Slatkin Galleries, New York; Royal
Trust Company, Montreal, 1962.

Jean-Honoré Fragonard probably drew this sheet in 1760–61, during or shortly
after his travels in Italy in the company of his patron the Abbé de Saint-Non
and the artist Hubert Robert. Toward the end of his stay at the Académie de France
in Rome, from 1756 to 1761, the young artist resided at the Villa d'Este on the out-
skirts of Rome, and visited Naples and Bologna where he drew monuments and
works of art at the request of the Abbé. Fragonard brought back hundreds of
sketches in red or black chalk from this trip, including copies after the great masters of the Baroque as well as drawings of the monuments of Antiquity.[1]

From a technical and stylistic standpoint, the rendering of the Ottawa drawing suggests a bas-relief, with the modelling achieved by marked contrasts between
heavy lines or darkened areas and the reserves of the paper. Although his subject
is of classical inspiration, the drawing is unrelated to any known monument. A similar pastiche of an antique relief is also found in the copies of ancient ruins and
decorative motifs that Fragonard executed in 1761. Eunice Williams holds the view
that the drawing in Ottawa is likely a fantastic interpretation, an exploratory study
on the theme of sacrifice whose end result is the piece Fragonard submitted for his
entry to the Académie, *The Sacrifice of Coreseus*, 1765, in the Louvre, which illustrates

FIG 38 Jean-Honoré Fragonard,
The Sacrifice of Coreseus, The Pierpont
Morgan Library, New York

FIG 39 Joseph-Marie Vien,
A Priestess Burns Incense on a Tripod,
Musée des Beaux-Arts, Strasbourg

a tale of vengeance and sacrificial suicide.[2] A sketch for this large canvas (fig. 38) manifests the same spirit as the Ottawa drawing: in it, Fragonard depicts a tragic scene in which the gravity of the actions is expressed by the gestures of the protagonists. The accoutrements and architecture give a foretaste of the Neoclassicism that would become ubiquitous in the 1780s.

While the drapery and architectural details in *Medea Slaying Her Children* are signs of a style *à la grecque*, the tripod at the far right is an even more striking precursor of this vogue, and would reoccur in Joseph-Marie Vien's *A Priestess Burns Incense on a Tripod*, 1762 (fig. 39), exhibited at the 1763 Salon.[3] Note that Fragonard had already used the same scenic element in a sheet dated 1761, in the Destailleur album at the Fogg Museum, Cambridge, Massachusetts.[4]

Medea slaying her children was not a frequent subject in the eighteenth century, although Poussin had already used the theme during the previous century in two drawings now at Windsor Castle.[5] The episode of the infanticide takes place in Corinth, where Jason, husband of the witch-priestess Medea, falls in love with Glauce. Insane with rage, Medea kills Glauce and her father, then slays her own children fathered by Jason. Wittkower summarizes Fragonard's singular interpretation of the event as follows: Medea, about to kill her children, is held back by the spirit of Pity, while Madness, seated on a throne and waving a jester's staff, incites her to pursue her dire plan. The fleeing figures on the left are thought to represent Reason and Virtue.[6]

24

Jean-Honoré Fragonard
Grasse 1732–1806 Paris

*Saint Michael Finds Discord and Other Vices in a Convent: Illustration for Ariosto's
"Orlando Furioso," Canto XIV* c. 1785–90

Black chalk and brown wash,
39.3 × 25.9 cm (irreg.)
PURCHASED 1977
NO. 18939
PROVENANCE
Hippolyte Walferdin until 1880
(sale, Hôtel Drouot, Paris, March
1880, no. 228); Louis Roederer,
Reims, and Léon Olry-Roederer
until 1922; Dr. A.S.W. Rosenbach,
Philadelphia; Thomas Agnew and
Sons, London.

FIG 40 Jean-Honoré Fragonard, *Charlemagne Leads Angelica Away from Roland*, Art Gallery of Ontario, Toronto, Purchase, Walter C. Laidlaw Endowment, 1978

This sheet by Jean-Honoré Fragonard is from a series of more than 176 drawings intended to illustrate *Orlando Furioso* (fig. 40), the epic by the Italian court poet Ludovico Ariosto, which was first published in 1516.[1] Springing from the tradition of courtly love and set against a backdrop of religious war, the poem tells the story – with its tragic denouement – of Orlando, a Christian knight who is in love with the beautiful Eastern enchantress Angelica. The drawings, which are distinguished by their fluid and occasionally sketchy rendering, do not lend themselves well to engraving, although the indications mentioned by Rosenberg – a black line framing some compositions and the inscription of the artist's name in the upper part – reveal the purpose for which they were probably intended.[2] While scholars may be unsure of Fragonard's reason for undertaking this project, they agree nonetheless in dating the execution of the drawings to the 1780s,[3] after the resounding success of two engraved editions (dated 1773 for the Italian edition and 1775–83 for the French translation) in which Charles-Nicolas Cochin took an active part.[4]

Eunice Williams considers this composition one of the most abstract in the series.[5] Despite the tangled lines and summarily applied areas of wash, the work gives the impression of a skilfully orchestrated production that uses the vertical format to good advantage. Baroque in spirit, the drawing places in opposition the dominant heavenly forces in the upper portion and the earthly world, site of vice and corruption, in the lower register. Within a monumental architectural frame, Saint Michael, at the upper right, discovers a monk with his hand in the alms box at the lower left; at the extreme right is a dishevelled nun, the embodiment of Discord; at his feet, in the guise of a pig and a peacock, are Gluttony and Pride. By his spirited and elaborate graphic treatment of the background, Fragonard succeeds in evoking the chaos prevailing in the convent.[6]

With the same painterly brio, Fragonard created a large number of illustrations for series such as the fables of La Fontaine. Although some of these images were begun as early as 1773, during Fragonard's stay in Italy, they were not engraved until 1795. A set of drawings for *Don Quixote*, like the series inspired by *Orlando Furioso*, would remain unfinished.[7]

25

JEAN-BAPTISTE LALLEMAND
Dijon 1716–1803 Paris

View of the Colosseum, Rome c. 1747–64

In this drawing, Jean-Baptiste Lallemand represents the Colosseum as seen from the Arch of Constantine. Built during the reign of Vespasian and known as the Flavian Amphitheatre, this Roman monument was long the scene of bloody spectacles and gladiatorial combats until they were banned by the emperor Honorius in the year 404. The Colosseum, which has been commonly known by that name since the Middle Ages, would then serve as a marble quarry until it was consecrated by Pope Benedict XIV in 1744 in memory of the Christians martyred in the arena.

Born in Dijon, Lallemand spent most of his professional life in Rome where he was renowned for his views of antique monuments, evidence of the Eternal City's past. He also made drawings of a large number of sites in his native land, including views of Burgundy, the Franche-Comté, and the area around Lyons, which were engraved for the twelve-volume *Voyage pittoresque de la France* (1781–96). Formerly attributed to Giovanni Marieschi, this picturesque view of the Colosseum shows the determining influence of the *vedutisti* on Lallemand; other works initially attributed to Giovanni Paolo Panini would later be revealed as Lallemand's work.[1] Marianne Roland Michel has also established definite affinities with a drawing by J.R. Cozens, one of Lallemand's English counterparts in Rome.[2] Note also that during his stay in Rome, Lallemand taught drawing to the young Robert Adam,[3] later one of Britain's most distinguished architects. An even clearer sign of Lallemand's kinship with these English artists was the fact that he exhibited at the London Society of Artists in 1773.

The drawing in Ottawa manifests the "delicacy" characteristic of Lallemand's drawings in wash and watercolour, as described by Quarré.[4] In the context of the revival of interest in Antiquity spurred by the excavations of Pompeii and Herculaneum, however, Lallemand's work remains of note rather for its archaeological content, which was the reason he was one of the artists whose name was proposed to Lord Elgin in 1799 to draw Greek monuments threatened with destruction.[5] Although this *View of the Colosseum* encourages us to assume a certain veracity, Lallemand's work is in general marked by a pronounced taste for the fantastic. In this respect, a parallel can be drawn with the compositions of Hubert Robert, with whom Lallemand doubtless rubbed shoulders in the circle of resident artists at the Académie de France in Rome, although Lallemand himself was never associated with that institution.[6]

Pen and brown ink with brown,
grey, and blue wash over traces of
black chalk, laid down,
15.6 × 27.5 cm
PURCHASED 1963
NO. 15009
INSCRIPTION
At upper left, *JL*
PROVENANCE
Robert Low (L. 2222); Colnaghi,
London, no. 36 in sale catalogue.

26
CHARLES-LOUIS CLÉRISSEAU
Paris 1722–1820 Auteuil
Peasants before the Arch of Sergius near Pola c. 1757

FIG 41 Charles-Louis Clérisseau, *The Arch of Sergius near Pola*, State Hermitage Museum, Saint Petersburg

FIG 42 Giovanni Antonio Canaletto, *Capriccio with a Roman Triumphal Arch*, The Metropolitan Museum of Art, New York, Harris Brisbane Dick Fund, 1946

Gouache, mounted, 40.9 × 58 cm

PURCHASED 1976

NO. 18698

INSCRIPTION

At lower right, *Clérisseau*

PROVENANCE

James Knapp-Fisher, Esq.; sale, Christie's, London, 30 March 1976, no. 146; Kate de Rothschild Gallery, London.

Architect and *ruiniste* (painter of ruins), Charles-Louis Clérisseau executed this gouache after a stay near Pola (today Pula) in Croatia while travelling with his Scottish pupil Robert Adam.[1] On that journey, the master captured the region's monuments in sketches he later used for a group of twenty-five finished works, in particular seven painted versions of the Arch of Sergius. According to McCormack, the version now in the Hermitage (fig. 41) inspired the subsequent variations, including the example in the National Gallery of Canada.[2] Around 1766, some of Clérisseau's compositions would suggest a series of fourteen engravings to Domenico Cugeno.[3]

Clérisseau's work would have a major influence on his contemporaries, both artists and art lovers, who appreciated his emphasis on picturesque views of the monuments of Antiquity, which were the source of the vogue for Neoclassical architecture. We can read Hubert Robert's reminiscences of Clérisseau's work; and even Giovanni Canaletto, his elder, would be inspired by his drawings, as evidenced by Canaletto's view of the Arch of Sergius at the Metropolitan Museum of Art (fig. 42).[4] Esteemed by the English and American elite, Clérisseau also obtained the favour of Catherine II of Russia in 1780: she invited him to design an arch of triumph in Saint Petersburg, but it would never be built.[5]

27
Louis-Nicolas de Lespinasse

Pouilly-sur-Loire 1734–1808 Nièvre

View of the Admiralty and Its Surroundings, Looking towards the West from the Triumphal Gate c. 1750–60

Pen and grey and brown ink and watercolour over traces of graphite, with touches of opaque white and gouache, 21.7 × 32.4 cm

PURCHASED 1968

NO. 15713

INSCRIPTIONS

On the recto, lower left, in pen and black ink, *D. L.*; on the verso, centre, in pen and brown ink, *Vue de l'Amirauté et de Ses Environs, en regardant de la porte triomphale Vers l'occident*

PROVENANCE

Private collection, Paris; Ader and Picard, March 1968; sale, Palais Galliera, Paris, 3 April 1968, no. 201; Galerie L'Œil, Paris.

This panoramic view of the Admiralty in Saint Petersburg and its larger companion drawing (fig. 43) demonstrate a manner of execution worthy of topographical images, in which accuracy and attention to detail predominate. Louis-Nicolas de Lespinasse was introduced to watercolour in the course of his military training and immediately showed an aptitude for the technique. He soon specialized in architectural and picturesque views, a large number of which would be engraved, but he was not admitted to the Académie until 1787.

As Sloan has already emphasized, it is unlikely that the Ottawa drawings were the result of an actual stay in Saint Petersburg.[1] Instead, Lespinasse was probably inspired by engravings made by Michail Ivanovic Machaev and published in 1753 on the occasion of the city's fiftieth anniversary.[2] Despite some noticeable differences between Lespinasse's drawings and Machaev's prints — views captured from closer up or further away, variations in the placement of figures, or ships that break up the open spaces — it is clear that the same slightly off-centre viewpoint is used in both. In depicting the Admiralty, Lespinasse truncated the building at the far right of the sheet, namely the Winter Palace, originally designed by Domenico Tressini and rebuilt between 1754 and 1762 under the direction of Bartolomeo Rastrelli. This omission supports the hypothesis that the young watercolourist executed his version during the 1750s, and chose not to include that part of the city because of the major reconstruction under way there. But it is still quite possible that Lespinasse's drawings were made long after these architectural modifications. About 1790, Claude Niquet engraved a *View of the Admiralty* in which he reproduced Lespinasse's composition exactly, even faithfully transferring the groups of figures to the print (fig. 44).

Two other panoramas of Saint Petersburg and a *View of Kazan*, 1768, with almost identical dimensions and the same meticulous graphic style, appeared on the market recently.[3] A clear connection can be established with a wash drawing by Lespinasse, *The Docks on the Neva*, circa 1770, in the Bibliothèque nationale, Paris.[4] There is no doubt that the drawings in Ottawa were part of a larger group intended to illustrate various physical and architectural aspects of the capital of the Tsars under Catherine II.

FIG 43 Louis-Nicolas de Lespinasse, *View of Saint Petersburg Looking up the Neva, with the Winter Palace*, NGC

VUE DE L'AMIRAUTÉ ET DE SES ENVIRONS.

FIG 44 Claude Niquet, *View of the Admiralty and Its Environs*, NGC

28
HUBERT ROBERT
Paris 1733–1808 Paris

Interior of a Funerary Temple, Inspired by the Mausoleum of Marcus Agrippa in Rome 1776

Red chalk, mounted on thick laid
paper, 36.9 × 28.9 cm
PURCHASED 1938
NO. 4445
ANNOTATION
At lower left, on the secondary
support, *Robert 1776*
PROVENANCE
Blind stamp, on lower-right corner
of sheet, *FR* (L. suppl. 1042); Galerie
Gilbert Levy, Paris.

FIG 45 Hubert Robert,
*The Mausoleum of Marcus Agrippa
in Rome*, location unknown

The subject of this red chalk drawing by Hubert Robert is related to that of a
larger sheet attributed to Robert and sold at auction in Paris in 1990 (fig. 45).[1]
Both show the same manner of delineating contrasts of light and shadow: the foreground planes, which are dark, are enhanced by the application of heavier and lighter
hatching; while the details of the background, which is bathed in light, are rendered
in delicate, sketchy lines. Under the arch of the great structure, figures are gathered around a tomb bearing the inscription MARCO AGRIPPA on its base, indicating
the location. The architecture and the outline of the tomb differ markedly in the
two works, however.

Such variations on a single theme are not unusual for Robert, who well after
his sojourn in Rome in 1765 was still reusing the celebrated motifs from the architecture of Antiquity which would contribute to his renown.[2] That being the case,
the date of 1776 on the support is credible, although the actual annotation may be
in the hand of one François Renaud, who mounted drawings and prints in Paris
during the same period.[3]

Several famous examples are extant of the views of Roman monuments that
Robert drew long after his visit. These include nine pen and watercolour drawings
on which Diderot commented on the occasion of the 1781 Salon, including a
Temple of Marcus Agrippa, dated 1780 and later described in greater detail by Charles
Sterling.[4] Ekaterina Deriabina has inventoried a drawing of the same subject,
signed and dated 1761, at present in the Musée des Beaux-Arts in Lyon; this is most
probably a preparatory study for a painting done in 1762–63, whose current location is unknown.[5]

29

LOUIS-GABRIEL MOREAU (THE ELDER)
Paris 1740–1805 Paris

Ruins of a Fortified Town c. 1760–65

Watercolour over traces of black
chalk, laid down, 16.1 × 24.2 cm
PURCHASED 1963
NO. 15010
WATERMARK
In the centre, *RVK & ALW*
PROVENANCE
Colnaghi, London.

Louis-Gabriel Moreau (called Moreau the Elder), an artist who specialized in bucolic scenes and antique ruins, was also a skilled etcher.[1] After an apprenticeship with Pierre Antoine de Machy, he began producing landscapes with ruins, in watercolour over traces of black chalk, as early as 1760.[2] As in the present sheet, he used a palette of light colours in these picturesque views, which are distinguished by effects of light arising from the contrast between broad surfaces of wash for the background and scattered dark touches representing areas in shadow. The scene is punctuated by figures simply suggested by brushstrokes of the proper scale.

In its subject and treatment, this watercolour reflects the pre-romantic sensibility that evolved during the second half of the eighteenth century. It is possible here to discern the influence of the writings of Jean-Jacques Rousseau and Salomon Gessner, which can also be seen in the contemporary enthusiasm in France for picturesque gardens, as Claude-Henri Watelet's *Essai sur les jardins*, published in 1774, confirms.

The 18th Century

Gallant Subjects and Genre Scenes

30
JEAN-ANTOINE WATTEAU
Valenciennes 1684–1721 Nogent-sur-Marne
Two Studies of Mezzetino Standing c. 1717

Red chalk, 17.7 × 18.9 cm

PURCHASED 1939

NO. 4548

PROVENANCE

Antoine-Joseph Dezallier
d'Argenville, no. 3270, and initials
in brown ink at lower right (L. 2951
under Crozat); his sale, Paris, 18–28
January 1779, part of lot 392 or 393;
Lenglier; Mme de Saint? (according
to the inscription on the old
frame); H.M. Calmann, London.

FIG 46 Jean-Antoine Watteau, *Meeting in the Open Air*, Staatliche
Kunstsammlungen Dresden, Gemäldegalerie Alte Meister

In this red chalk drawing, Jean-Antoine Watteau presents a model dressed in the manner of Mezzetino, the amorous valet of the commedia dell'arte, from two different angles. Such multiple representations of a subject on a single sheet were not uncommon for Watteau, whose light, rapid strokes successfully capture both fabric texture and anatomical details. While the figure on the right is executed in loose, freely drawn lines, the one on the left presents a more finished appearance, especially in the facial features and the rendering of the garments. Parker and Mathey associate the left-hand figure with a study for *Meeting in the Open Air* (fig. 46).[1] The relation between the Ottawa drawing and the Dresden painting is evident, but in the final version the artist chose to picture the model in a frontal rather than a back view, in the lower-left area of the canvas. The painting dates to 1717–18, shortly after Watteau was admitted to the Académie with the title *peintre de fêtes galantes*, referring to his reception piece *The Embarkation from Cythera*, now in the Louvre.

Originally owned by Dezallier d'Argenville, the drawing carries the erudite amateur's initials and characteristic collection numbering at the lower right.[2] The Mezzetino on the left appears in the same stance in a crayon manner engraving by Jean-Charles François,[3] the fifth in a series of six made after drawings by Watteau once in Dezallier d'Argenville's collection. The plates were later acquired by Gilles Demarteau, whose nephew Gilles-Antoine retouched four of them, notably the Mezzetino to which he added a landscape background (fig. 47).[4]

FIG 47 Gilles-Antoine Demarteau, *Mezzetino Standing, Seen from the Back in Three-Quarter View*, Bibliothèque nationale, Paris

31
CLAUDE GILLOT
Langres 1673–1722 Paris
Rocky Grotto c. 1715

Pen and brown ink with brown
wash, 15.4 × 20 cm
PURCHASED 1973
NO. 17650
WATERMARK
Partial, *E*, four-leaf clover, *CAMBON*
INSCRIPTION
At lower left, toward the centre
Gillot
PROVENANCE
Brigadier F.P. Barclay; sale,
Christie's, London, 26 November
1973, no. 288; Richard Day.

Fine parallel lines, drawn as though incised, lend this pen and brown ink drawing a resemblance to an etching.[1] Claude Gillot produced several drawings of this type, similar in size and graphic characteristics, for the cycle of seventeen capriccios engraved by the Count of Caylus.[2] Five of these drawings, formerly in the Calando collection, came onto the Parisian art market in 1970.[3] The Museum of Fine Arts Boston possesses a *Mascarade* (fig. 48) of comparable style, and a mended and redrawn portion of it relates it to the Ottawa sheet.[4] In the Ottawa work, the group of figures at the extreme left is a later addition: the artist modified the initial image by cutting out a window and pasting a piece of the same paper on the verso; he then drew the figures in the original ink. A line of greenish-black ink frames the drawing, and the identical ink has been used to accentuate certain compositional details, including the tree trunk and the entrance to the grotto.[5]

The Ottawa drawing contains all the features of a landscape, yet this genre is fairly rare in Gillot's oeuvre. The dominant motif of the hollowed-out rocky crag, surmounted by vegetation, reveals evident Flemish sources to which Gillot could have been exposed through engravings.[6] This type of grandiose fantasy landscape, with a natural arch and tiny human figures, is common to numerous picturesque views in sixteenth- and seventeenth-century Flemish art. One example is a painting by Cornelis van Dalem, *The Flight into Egypt in a Rocky Landscape* (fig. 49), which features a monumental arch attractively overhung with vegetation, at the foot of which sit figures of Oriental appearance. Another graphic, and iconographic,

FIG 48 Claude Gillot, *Mascarade*, The Museum of Fine Arts Boston, The Forsyth Wickes Collection

connection can be made with an etching by Hieronymus Cock, *Landscape with Leander Swimming the Hellespont* (fig. 50). Both Gillot's drawing and Cock's print feature the use of fine, generally tight hatching to render the shadows. And although the background massif is given less importance in the etching, the two swans on the water and the reeds along the bank are echoed in the Ottawa drawing.

Such consistency and minute detail give the work an overly refined quality not unlike the *rocaille* style that Gillot was one of the first to adopt. Initially trained as a draughtsman by his father, an embroidery designer and ornament painter, Gillot specialized in set design and genre scenes. He explored the grotesque genre in a red chalk composition, *The Feast of Pan*, 1707–08, in the Musée des Beaux-Arts de Lille.[7] The backdrop of the Lille sheet features two grottos arranged in perfect symmetry, one on either side of a herm of Pan. The rocky element has been transformed into a stage set and the characters have taken their places. In spirit this drawing can be compared to the Ottawa sheet, where Gillot exploits the decorative potential of the rocky motif.

FIG 49 Cornelis Van Dalem, *The Flight into Egypt in a Rocky Landscape*, Staatliche Museen zu Berlin, Preussischer Kulturbesitz, Gemäldegalerie

FIG 50 Hieronymus Cock, *Landscape with Leander Swimming the Hellespont*, British Museum, London

32
NICOLAS LANCRET
Paris 1690–1743 Paris

Guitar Player VERSO: *Sketch of Groups of Soldiers, and a Soldier Carrying a Package* (not illustrated) c. 1725–30

Red chalk touched with darker shade of red chalk, 23.9 × 11.6 cm
PURCHASED 1951
NO. 6048
PROVENANCE
Charles Drouet; Thomas Agnew and Sons Ltd., London.

FIG 51 Jean Audran, *Figures of Various Characters* (no. 187), Bibliothèque nationale, Paris

FIG 52 François Boucher, *A Young Man Standing, Frontal View, Playing a Tamboura*, Musée du Louvre, Département des arts graphiques, Collection Edmond de Rothschild, Paris

FIG 53 G. Scottin, *Greek from the Islands of the Archipelago Playing a Tamboura*, Bibliothèque nationale, Paris

This study of an elegantly costumed musician relates to none of Nicolas Lancret's known paintings. He may have created it as a simple exercise, or perhaps to please a patron.[1] The guitarist, depicted here in an iconic pose, was an important figure in the *fête galante* painting tradition, abundantly used by Watteau and later Lancret, "to accompany or substitute for tender confidences."[2]

The subject of *Guitar Player* is consistent with the rigid figures in constricted poses of Lancret's drawings, distinguishable from those of Watteau, his master, by a hand that is at times awkward or hesitant. According to Wintermute, this sheet dates to a few years after Watteau's death, while his dominance was still manifesting itself in the form of entertainers, musicians, and actors peopling the work of his followers.[3] Watteau's influence in the Ottawa example can be traced in particular to the guitar-playing Pierrot that he drew for the series *Figures of Various Characters*, engraved by Jean Audran around 1735 (fig. 51). In both cases, the guitarist is motionless and isolated, captured in a frontal pose.

A still more evident relationship exists with *A Young Man Standing, Frontal View, Playing a Tamboura*, engraved by François Boucher after Watteau (fig. 52), whose own source was plainly an engraving by G. Scottin executed around 1715 after Jean-Baptiste Van Mour (fig. 53).[4] Watteau largely plagiarized the musician theme, specifically the guitarist, but, as Mirimonde points out,[5] his transcriptions are differentiated by their quality. Lancret brings originality to his copy by replacing the Oriental iconography with the attributes of a courtier.[6] However, the feet placed at right angles and the ample costume that suggests a pear-shaped body remain the same.

33

PIERRE-ANTOINE QUILLARD
Paris 1710–1733 Lisbon

Fête Galante in a Park VERSO: *Three Small Compositional Sketches* (not illustrated) c. 1725

Red chalk, 17.9 × 28 cm
PURCHASED 1999
NO. 40095
PROVENANCE
E. Dervaux; sale, Sotheby's,
Monaco, 15 June 1990, lot 47;
Thomas Le Claire Kunsthandel,
Hamburg.

Like many other red chalk drawings by Pierre-Antoine Quillard, this sheet was once attributed to Jean-Antoine Watteau, his elder.[1] Thus it is not surprising to find quotations drawn directly from the master's paintings. For example, the couple at the far right recalls a similar motif in *The Enchanted Isle*, in a Swiss private collection, while the young woman being helped to her feet by a courtly gentleman is found in *The Embarkation from Cythera*.[2] The lady and the insistent courtier seated by a fountain in the middle ground resemble one of the couples in *The Conversation*, but Colin Bailey sees a still more direct source in Jean-François de Troy's canvas *The Declaration of Love*, which he supposes Quillard to have seen at the 1725 Salon.[3]

This compositional study does not relate to any known painting or engraving by Quillard. However, it exhibits the formal characteristics typical of the artist's late work: figures with fine and occasionally angular faces captured in gracious poses, and orderly hatching that creates an overall rhythm. From a stylistic perspective, Wintermute associates this drawing with a red chalk *Fête Galante* in the Louvre (fig. 54).[4] In some respects, though, the Ottawa sheet has a more finished appearance, comparable to the courtship scene held in the Ricardo do Espírito Santo Silva foundation in Lisbon.[5]

Little is known about this artist even today, other than that he died at the age of twenty-three and earned his reputation by becoming painter to the king of Portugal in 1727, while still an adolescent.[6] *Fête Galante in a Park* illustrates the work of a young draughtsman and promising painter who applied the principles developed by his elders, carrying on the *rocaille* tradition.

FIG 54 Pierre-Antoine Quillard, *Fête Galante*, Musée du Louvre, Cabinet des dessins, Paris

34

FRANÇOIS BOUCHER
Paris 1703–1770 Paris

Studies of the Head and Hands of a Seated Boy for "Of Three Things, Will You Do One for Me?"
VERSO: *Study of the Same Boy Seated on a Chair* c. 1733

Red and white chalks on brown
laid paper, with border in pen and
black ink; verso, red and white
chalks, 35 × 26.9 cm
PURCHASED 1983
NO. 28217
ANNOTATIONS
At lower left, in pen and brown
ink, *Cardin*, over *Boucher* in black
chalk
PROVENANCE
Tan Bunzl-de Rothschild, London.

This sheet of studies provides a chance to appreciate the work of the young François Boucher as he developed the oval painting *Of Three Things, Will You Do One for Me?* (fig. 55).[1] A later variation of the canvas served as a model for an engraving by Jacques-Jean Pasquier which appeared in 1768 (fig. 56); Pasquier also engraved a pendant, *Elle Mord à la Grappe (She Takes a Bite of the Bunch of Grapes)*, which has vanished.[1] The line in this drawing, at once fluid and assured, is also evident in a sheet portraying a boy holding an egg (fig. 57), executed during the same period. During the 1730s, Boucher created a number of pastoral pictures in the same format, all with subjects containing an implicit sexual connotation.[2]

While McAllister Johnson sees in the sketch on the verso an independent drawing evocative of Chardin's work,[3] Mimi Cazort considers the study of the young man seated on a chair, seen in three-quarter view from behind, to be the first in the series. According to this hypothesis, with which Françoise Joulie agrees, Boucher went on to experiment further on the other side of the sheet, drawing the same figure in profile from a closer viewpoint and concentrating separately on details of the facial expression and the hands.[4] In the finished work, the insistent young suitor is depicted, not seated, but discernibly kneeling at the girl's feet; moreover, even though the Ottawa drawing provides a fairly definite solution for the head of the young gallant, the position of the hands is still vague. As Rosenberg has pointed out, the young man in the pastel drawing *Young Man Holding a Parsnip*, at the Art Institute of Chicago, resembles the youth in the oval painting,[5] so there is reason to believe that the pastel and the sheet in Ottawa derive from the same model.

FIG 55 François Boucher, *Of Three Things, Will You Do One for Me?*, Fondation Ephrussi-de-Rothschild, Saint-Jean-Cap-Ferrat

FIG 56 Jacques-Jean Pasquier, *Of Three Things, Will You Do One for Me?*, Musée du Louvre, Département des arts graphiques, Collection Edmond de Rothschild, Paris

FIG 57 François Boucher, *Boy Holding an Egg*, Fogg Art Museum, Harvard University Art Museums, Gift of Agnes Mongan

RECTO

VERSO

35
François Boucher
Paris 1703–1770 Paris
Study for "The Country Meal" c. 1730

Red chalk, laid down, 32.3 × 23.7 cm
PURCHASED 1938
NO. 4444
PROVENANCE
M. de Beer, London.

FIG 58 François Boucher,
The Country Meal, private collection,
Germany

Once ascribed to Jacques-Philippe Le Bas, this pastoral, with its vigorous use of line, was recognized in 1963 by Denise Cailleux-Mégret as being the work of the young Boucher.[1] John Ruch and Pierre Rosenberg independently supported this attribution, which was confirmed in 1984 by the discovery of the corresponding Boucher painting, *The Country Meal* (fig. 58).[2]

Alastair Laing demonstrated the originality of Boucher's *pastorales*: certain literary works inspired the painter to set his stage with shepherds and shepherdesses in a bucolic setting, on a note of sentimental fantasy.[3] But the true ancestry of *The Country Meal* and its preliminary drawing at the National Gallery of Canada can be found in the rustic scenes of Dutch art, in particular those of Abraham Bloemaert. Moreover, Rosenberg has drawn a parallel with another Boucher painting, *Country Life*, which manifests a similar spirit and most probably dates to shortly after Boucher's stay in Rome in the early 1730s.[4] Some of the figures in *Country Life* can be identified easily from Boucher engravings in the *Livre d'Étude d'après les Desseins Originaux de Blomart* (1735), which illustrates scenes from everyday life;[5] the current drawing and the related painting suggest the same source, although it has not yet been possible to determine the identities of the models. Rosenberg also maintains that the rather mannered style of *The Country Meal* and the monumentality of the figures are further evidence that its execution goes back to Boucher's time in Rome, effectively dating the drawing in Ottawa to the same period. Françoise Joulie confirms this hypothesis in linking the standing woman's position and hairstyle to a Boucher copy after Solimena in Ajaccio.

36

FRANÇOIS BOUCHER
Paris 1703–1770 Paris

Design for a Fan: Bacchus and Ariadne c. 1749

Red, white and black chalks,
laid down, 22.6 × 43.5 cm
PURCHASED 1960
NO. 9071
INSCRIPTION
At bottom centre, *françois Bouché*
PROVENANCE
Colnaghi, London.

The story of Bacchus and Ariadne, inspired by a passage from Ovid's *Metamorphoses* (Book VIII), was a popular theme among French artists of the seventeenth and eighteenth centuries. According to the myth, Bacchus weds Ariadne, whom he finds asleep after Theseus has abandoned her on the island of Naxos. About 1793, Antoine Coypel created a painting of the subject for the Duke of Orleans, thus setting the tone for a mythology of *galanterie* that would reach its full flowering in the eighteenth century (fig. 59).[1] The masterpiece inspired a large number of copies and subsequent versions, among which François Boucher's interpretation might well be numbered.

With an energetic, vigorous line, Boucher chooses to place the two protagonists in the centre, surrounded by nymphs and Cupids, against a background of classical architecture. The composition around a semicircle immediately suggests the destination of the work: a painted fan.[2] Boucher's contribution to the decorative arts was primarily to tapestry-making: starting in 1736, he provided numerous cartoons for the Beauvais manufactory, and later for the Gobelins, where he became inspector in 1755. His best-known commission was undoubtedly the one he executed for the series *The Loves of the Gods*, whose first subject was Bacchus and Ariadne. Although the cartoon was already made by 1747, this first tapestry in the series would not be woven until 1749.[3]

While the composition of both the drawing in Ottawa and the tapestry, a portion of which can be found in the Metropolitan Museum of Art (fig. 60), is based on a semicircle, with architectural elements in the background, the placement of the figures differs in the two versions, their position being reversed with respect to the central axis. It is reasonable to suppose that the drawing preceded the tapestry and perhaps even its cartoon, which has since disappeared, but this conjecture, which dates the drawing circa 1745–47, remains to be verified.

FIG 60 Tapestry, Beauvais (18th century), *Bacchus and Ariadne, from a set of the Loves of the Gods*, The Metropolitan Museum of Art, New York, From the Collection of James Stillman, Gift of Ernest G. Stillman, 1922

FIG 59 Antoine Coypel, *Bacchus and Ariadne on the Island of Naxos*, Philadelphia Museum of Art

37

Pierre-Antoine Baudouin
Paris 1723–1769 Paris
Bringing the Bride to Bed 1767

Gouache over red chalk and traces
of graphite, 36 × 31.7 cm
PURCHASED 1984
NO. 28441
INSCRIPTION
At lower right, in pen and brown
ink, *Baudouin*
PROVENANCE
R.M. Light & Co., Santa Barbara,
California, 1984.

Straddling the line between *galanterie* and eroticism, this gouache study illustrates the initial moments of the wedding night of a well-born bride and her imploring young bridegroom, with ladies-in-waiting bustling about them. The finished work, also in gouache, was done on the occasion of the marriage of the Marquis de Marigny, brother of the Marquise de Pompadour. In his comments on the Salon of 1767, Diderot included a lengthy criticism of the composition, which he judged to be "of inferior taste" and light morals, when contrasted with the virtuous scenes depicted by Greuze.[1] Although the work exhibited at the Salon has disappeared, there exists an obvious concordance between Diderot's description and the study presented here.[2] Later, Jean-Michel Moreau and Jean-Baptiste Simonet would engrave the scene for the Count of Hautefort, Marquis de Villacerf, as the arms and inscription in the lower part indicate (fig. 61). According to the custom of the time, the issuing of the print was announced in the *Mercure de France* in September 1770. Its pendant, on the theme *The Bride Arising*, would be engraved by Philippe Trière after the work of Jean Démosthène Dugourc.[3]

McAllister Johnson has already described the differences between the gouache in Ottawa and the engraved version, stressing the different destinations of the two works; the first was intended for the private approval of the Marquis, the second for public dissemination.[4] According to Johnson, the gouache contains a very particular iconography that gives us information about the person who commissioned it: above the door is a shield on which the letter *M* and two intertwined hearts can be seen, and on the mantelpiece stands a statue representing *Love and Marriage United by Friendship*, one of the preferred subjects of the King's favourite.[5] The decoration under the young bridegroom's arm, moreover, appears to be the Order of Saint Louis. In the engraving, part of a different commission, all such references to the original recipient of the drawing were removed. Note that in 2002 a painting appeared on the market, signed "Mulnier peintre du Roy" (Mulnier, painter to the King); it is similar to the engraving in every detail.[6]

FIG 61 Jean-Michel Moreau and
Jean-Baptiste Simonet, *Bringing the Bride
to Bed*, Bibliothèque nationale, Paris

38
JEAN-BAPTISTE OUDRY
Paris 1686–1755 Beauvais

"The Torrent and the River," from a Series Designed to Illustrate the "Fables" of La Fontaine 1732

Brush and black and grey wash, heightened with opaque white, on blue laid paper, 31.1 × 25.9 cm
PURCHASED 1981
NO. 26551
INSCRIPTION
At lower left, *JB Oudry / 1732*
PROVENANCE
For the early history, see *J.-B. Oudry 1686–1755*, exh. cat., Galeries nationales du Grand Palais, Paris, 1982, p. 157; Louis Olry-Roederer, Rheims, France; Rosenbach Company, New York, 1923; Raphaël Esmerian, New York, 1946; sale of his library, 3rd part, Palais Galliera, Paris, 6 June 1973, no. 46; Dr. Claus Virch, Paris.

This brush and wash drawing, with white gouache highlights on blue paper, is part of a suite of 276 sheets, including the frontispiece, executed by Jean-Baptiste Oudry between 1729 and 1734 to illustrate La Fontaine's *Fables*.[1] Like other scholars before him, Opperman stresses the fact that Oudry used motifs drawn from earlier illustrated books inspired by Aesop's fables.[2]

The Ottawa drawing is from the second *Fables* album by Oudry, sold at auction in 1973.[3] The album was broken up after the sale, and the drawings are now dispersed in numerous private and public collections in Europe and North America.[4] All the same size and bordered in blue ink wash, they are notable for a highly painterly style. Oudry portrays the animals with a verisimilitude unmatched in the series engraved between 1755 and 1759 after the line drawings by Cochin (see cat. 39).[5] *The Torrent and the River* demonstrates his talent as an animal artist in the detail of the horse's head in the foreground, rendered with minimal brushstrokes, and in the representation of the setting.

In the tale of *The Torrent and the River*, a traveller is forced to cross a fearsome raging torrent to flee a band of brigands. Unharmed, and encouraged by his feat, he continues on, and when the robbers again approach he steers his mount into the seemingly calm waters of a river, never suspecting the danger of its deadly current. Oudry pictures the traveller and his horse just as they are disappearing into the deep. The moral of the fable, in the words of a proverb, is: Beware of silent dogs and still waters.

39

CHARLES-NICOLAS COCHIN
Paris 1715–1790 Paris
"The Cobbler and the Financier," for "Selected Fables" by La Fontaine (vol. III, fable CXLIV) c. 1755

C harles-Nicolas Cochin[1] directed the production of a deluxe edition of La Fontaine's *Fables* that was issued between 1755 and 1759 on the initiative of Louis Regnard de Montenault, a La Fontaine enthusiast who had acquired the 276 wash and gouache drawings on blue paper made by Jean-Baptiste Oudry between 1729 and 1734 (see cat. 38).[2] In 1751, Cochin began producing line drawings after the Oudry sheets, as their sometimes sketchy style was deemed inappropriate for an engraved adaptation. This monumental project, which would enjoy critical success only in the context of the Seven Years' War, required the work of forty-two engravers, whose proofs were corrected by Cochin.[3]

Like most of Cochin's sheets for the project, the Ottawa example bears the name of the designated engraver – in this case, Pierre Chenu – in the lower-right margin. Trained in the studio of Le Bas, Chenu practised etching and burin techniques and specialized in engraved reproductions of works by Flemish and Dutch painters. Despite his remarkable output, little is known about this craftsman, who signed thirteen of the *Fables* pieces, including *The Cobbler and the Financier* (fig. 62).[4] The location of Oudry's original drawing from 1731 is unknown.[5]

Cochin's *Cobbler and the Financier* has all the earmarks of a working drawing for an etching: squaring, numbered reference points in the margins, red chalk preparation on the verso, and incised outlines. These indications nicely illustrate the printmaking technique: prepared with red chalk on the verso, the sheet was placed on a varnished copper plate coated with white; the drawn lines on the recto were then traced with a stylus, transferring the red chalk equivalent to the plate. While all of Oudry's work for the *Fables* series is well known, Cochin's drawings for the later project only recently came to light, as noted by Marianne Roland Michel.[6] One is owned by the École nationale supérieure des beaux-arts in Paris, *The Joker and the Fishes*, and three others with similar characteristics appear in a 1991 Galerie Cailleux catalogue.[7] Beyond its didactic value in relation to the fable, the working drawing seen here sheds light on an essential step in the production of one of the most important engraved series of the eighteenth century.

FIG 62 Pierre Chenu, *The Cobbler and the Financier*, Bibliothèque nationale, Paris

Graphite, squared with stylus for
transfer; verso, red chalk,
28.4 × 22.1 cm
PURCHASED 2003
NO. 41139
WATERMARK
In the centre, *HR*, similar to
Heawood 3078
ANNOTATIONS
Numbered in upper and right
margins; at lower right, *chenu*
PROVENANCE
Michel Gierzod, Paris.

40

JEAN-BAPTISTE GREUZE
Tournus 1725–1805 Paris

Study of a Head of an Old Woman Wearing a Veil for "The Neapolitan Gesture" 1756

Red chalk, 25 × 19 cm
PURCHASED 2003
NO. 41259
INSCRIPTION
At lower right, in pen and red ink,
Greuze f. Roma anno 1756
PROVENANCE
Rabourdin and Choppin de Janvry
sale, Paris, 18 October 2002, no. 80;
Christophe de Quénetain, Paris.

This red chalk study representing the veiled head of an old woman is a preparatory drawing for *The Neapolitan Gesture* (fig. 63), executed during Jean-Baptiste Greuze's stay in Rome from 1755 to 1757.[1] Commissioned by Louis Gougenot, Abbot of Chezal-Benoît, the painting was exhibited at the 1757 Salon along with its pendant, *The Broken Eggs* (1756, The Metropolitan Museum of Art), for which Greuze used the same models. The critics of the day were charmed by the picturesque interpretation of the young woman's "Neapolitan gesture": she waves her fingers under her chin to signify the dismissal of her suitor, a Portuguese gentleman disguised as a peddler, unmasked by the old servant who recognizes the cross of nobility that he wears. The drawing captures the servant's expression as she discovers the deceit. Several drawings for the painting composition are extant,[2] including a study of the servant standing recently acquired by the J. Paul Getty Museum (fig. 64).[3] An engraving by Pierre-Étienne Moitte shown at the 1763 Salon attests the painting's success (fig. 65).

Study of a Head of an Old Woman, whose attribution to Greuze has been confirmed by Edgar Munhall,[4] is notable for the dramatic effect created by the shadow of the veil projected on the servant's face. Discreet, barely evoked with rough strokes, the veil allows the viewer's gaze to focus on the visage of the character, her every wrinkle finely and precisely drawn. As a general rule, Greuze rendered his models' expressions in red chalk, carefully representing the nuances of shade and light created by the subject's pose. His expressive heads, most often in large format, helped to establish his reputation as a proponent of moral genre painting. Some would give rise to engravings, such as his studies for *The Paralytic*, reproduced by Pierre-Charles Ingouf in 1766 for the series *Heads of Various Characters*.[5]

Drawings constitute a large part of Greuze's oeuvre, since he made numerous studies for his canvases. Testifying to the popularity of these sheets are more than 100 pieces held in the State Hermitage Museum in Saint Petersburg[6] and countless others dispersed in private and public collections around the world.

FIG 64 Jean-Baptiste Greuze, *Old Woman with Arms Outstretched*, J. Paul Getty Museum, Los Angeles, Gift of Joseph F. McCrindle

FIG 63 Jean-Baptiste Greuze, *The Neapolitan Gesture*, Worcester Art Museum, Mass., Charlotte E.W. Buffington Fund

FIG 65 Pierre-Étienne Moitte, *The Neapolitan Gesture*, NGC

41
JEAN-BAPTISTE LE PRINCE
Metz 1734–1781 Saint-Denis-du-Port

Hunters Resting 1777

FIG 66 Jean-Baptiste Le Prince, *Landscape with Figures*, Ashmolean Museum, Oxford

Brush and brown ink, and brown wash over black chalk, on cream laid paper, laid down on thin card, 23 × 29.8 cm

PURCHASED 1964

NO. 14500

INSCRIPTION

At lower left, *Le Prince 1777*

PROVENANCE

Hôtel Drouot, Paris, 25 May 1962, no. 51; Galerie Cailleux, Paris.

This landscape relates to several others of the same format and technique done in 1776–77, not long after Jean-Baptiste Le Prince presented his *Principes du dessin dans le genre du paysage* (1773) at the Académie. Given that he advocated direct study from nature, it is hardly surprising to detect reminders of such pre-Romantic artists as Francesco Giuseppe Casanova or Philippe-Jacques de Loutherbourg in his work.[1] Here, diluted sepia ink applied touch by touch with a brush results in a highly detailed scene that resembles an "engraving in the wash manner" – a technique that Le Prince invented. Other than the Ottawa example and a comparable work in the Ashmolean Museum (fig. 66), Whiteley notes similar drawings in many public collections including the Louvre, the Musée des Beaux-Arts d'Orléans, and the Metropolitan Museum of Art.[2]

The drawing under consideration is a late work by this artist, who was best known in his day for the Russian subjects criticized by Diderot in his Salon reviews.[3] Long after visiting the land of the tsars, Le Prince continued to revisit the themes that made him famous as illustrations for *A Journey into Siberia*, made in 1764–68.[4] Although this sheet dates to his twilight years in the French countryside, at Saint-Denis-du-Port, near Lagny, the figures in the foreground garbed *à la russe* testify to the profound influence of his Russian travels.

42

Jean-Baptiste Huet

Paris 1745–1811 Paris

Shepherd and His Flock Resting under the Trees 1771

Black chalk heightened with white chalk, laid down, 36.9 × 46.2 cm

PURCHASED 1963

NO. 15138

INSCRIPTION

In the lower-right quadrant, *J. B. Hüet 1771*

PROVENANCE

Hôtel Drouot, Paris, Étude Laurin, 28 March 1963; Galerie Cailleux, Paris.

Two years after being admitted to the Académie on the basis of his reception piece, *Dog Attacking Geese*, 1769, Jean-Baptiste Huet executed *Shepherd and His Flock Resting under the Trees*.[1] Judging by its finished appearance — with alternating black and white chalks creating subtle nuances of light and shade — this sheet may well have been shown at the 1771 Salon reviewed by Diderot.[2] Mimi Cazort raises the further possibility that the work was transposed to an engraving medium.[3] Note that in 1770, Huet produced a series of etchings dedicated to his master, Le Prince.[4] It also bears noting that many of Huet's drawings were engraved, in large part in the crayon manner, by his friend Demarteau but also by the artist himself, as etchings.

In some respects, this carefully rendered bucolic scene recalls the pastorals of François Boucher, but the sheep in the foreground, among other things, are utterly typical of the work of Huet, who specialized in drawn, engraved, and painted animal scenes. Indeed, it was as an animal painter that he would collaborate on the decoration for a room in the home of the engraver Gilles Demarteau. The few surviving canvases are held in the Musée Carnavalet. From 1783 until his death, Huet played an important role in the decorative arts, as seen in his work for the fabric manufacturer Christophe Philippe Oberkampf.[5]

The 18th and 19th Centuries

Neoclassicism and Romanticism

43

JACQUES LOUIS DAVID
Paris 1748–1825 Brussels

Portrait Assumed to be of Jean-Baptiste Robert Lindet 1795

Pen and black ink, with brush and
grey wash on traces of black chalk,
laid down, 19 cm in diameter
PURCHASED 1995
NO. 37846
INSCRIPTION
In the lower-left quadrant, _David_
PROVENANCE
Lady Abdy, Paris; sale, Hôtel
Drouot, Paris, 10 December 1993,
no. 15; W.M. Brady & Co., Inc.,
New York.

This portrait in the form of a medallion, rather in the spirit of antique busts, was part of a series of nine depictions of _Montagnard_ deputies, radical revolutionaries imprisoned in 1795. Jacques Louis David, jailed at the same time, immortalized the features of his companions in misfortune, using an intimist format; the drawings, which were inventoried by Rosenberg and Prat, are all round in shape, and vary between 17.6 and 19.3 centimetres in diameter.[1] The inscriptions on identified portraits, like the one of Jeanbon Saint-André in the collection of the Art Institute of Chicago, reveal David's friendship with and affection for his models.[2]

Like most of these drawings, the Ottawa sheet is surrounded by a border in green wash and bears a realistic, detailed rendering in which the greatest attention is paid to the subject's expression and individuality. Noteworthy are the delicate control of the wash and the economical but felicitous use of the pen, which follows the outlines drawn first in black chalk. In fact, this technical precision represents a nod to Neoclassicism, as does the pose of the model, captured with body in three-quarters view and head in profile, gaze directed upward in a noble attitude. The honourable and official – almost standard, one might say – character emanating from the portrait recalls the decorum of medals from Roman Antiquity and gives the subject historical weight.

The identity of the subject of this drawing is still not certain; initially, he was thought to be Jean-Baptiste Robert Lindet (1746–1825), lawyer and activist during the Reign of Terror, who became a parliamentarian and represented the Eure region at the time of the Convention. Like David, Robert Lindet had been a member of the Committee of Public Safety led by Maximilien Robespierre, who was guillotined in 1794. Rosenberg and Prat, however, were unable to reach the same conclusion when they compared this portrait with an engraving by Porreau that shows Robert Lindet as an older man.[3]

44
Jacques-Antoine-Marie Lemoine
Rouen 1751–1824 Paris

Portrait Assumed to be of Pierre-Victurnien Vergniaud before 1793

Black chalk and grey wash, heightened with white chalk, on wove paper, 26.9 × 19.9 cm

PURCHASED 1969
NO. 15759

PROVENANCE
René Fribourg; sale, Sotheby's, London, 16 October 1963, lot 581; Schidlof; Faerber and Maison, London.

FIG 67 Geoffroy, *Portrait of Vergniaud*, NGC

This portrait is one of the works inventoried by Jeffares in his 1999 catalogue, although the attribution to Jacques-Antoine-Marie Lemoine was unconfirmed.[1] The finesse of execution of the drawing, with its subtle blending of grey wash, stumped black chalk, and heightening in white chalk, attests long experience in drawing and full maturity as an artist. The naturalism and intensity of the sitter's glance is clearly reminiscent of the art of Maurice Quentin de La Tour, with whom Lemoine may have studied in the late 1770s.[2]

Portraitist and miniaturist, born into a bourgeois family in Rouen, Lemoine initially trained with Jean-Baptiste Descamps, then studied in Paris at the studio of Jean-Jacques Lagrenée (the Younger). From its beginning in the early 1770s and continuing on through the Revolution and after, his abundant work portrayed figures from all milieux – from the world of art, theatre, and music, from high society, and from the political arena. Examples from the last category are the portraits of Louis XVI, 1774, and Napoleon, 1801–02.[3]

The identification of the subject – Pierre-Victurnien Vergniaud – is based on the association with an engraving by Geoffroy (fig. 67), glued to the back of the frame when the work was acquired by the National Gallery of Canada. Born in Limoges in 1753, Vergniaud distinguished himself as a brilliant orator and parliamentarian, and played an active role in the early days of the Revolution. His controversial views, however, caused him to be brought before the revolutionary tribunal; he was sentenced to death in 1793, shortly after the tribunal had handed down the identical sentence to Louis XVI.[4]

45

JEAN-BAPTISTE-JOSEPH WICAR
Lille 1752–1834 Rome

Portrait of Atanasio Mousa of Epirus c. 1800

Black chalk, laid down on wove
paper, 17.4 × 17.5 cm
PURCHASED 2001
NO. 40670
INSCRIPTIONS
At upper left, *Attanasio Moussa /
d'Epiro*; upper right, *mort le 11.fe /
vrier / a Rome / ajer* [illegible] */ de
84 ans*; lower right, *Vicar fecit.*
PROVENANCE
Private collection, France; Thomas
Williams Fine Art Ltd., London.

In choosing a profile view and a realistic approach for his *Portrait of Atanasio Mousa of Epirus*, Jean-Baptiste-Joseph Wicar demonstrated a taste for the Neoclassical inherited from his master, Jacques Louis David.[1] Wicar's manner is recognizable by "the precision of the modelling obtained with fine, tight cross-hatching or hatching."[2] The Ottawa drawing was originally part of an album of drawings, since broken up; the known sheets, which are similar in format and style, are signed *Vicar fecit* at the lower right and all carry necrological inscriptions. In addition to the subject's name at the upper left, details of social condition, origin, or age appear at the upper right (figs. 68 and 69). Some of the artist's drawn portrait notebooks are in the collection of the Musée des Beaux-Arts de Lille[3] and in the Museo Napoleonico in Rome. Two others were sold at auction in London in 1971 and in 1998.[4]

Even with the inscription, virtually the only facts known about the subject of the Ottawa sheet, Atanasio Mousa, are that he was from Epirus, a region straddling the Albanian-Greek border, and that he died in Rome on 11 February, in an undetermined year, at the age of eighty-four. His appearance is that of a somewhat younger man, implying that the inscription was added at a later time. His casual dress – to judge by the headgear – suggests that he was likely sketched in his home. He may have been the owner of the Café d'Atanasio in Rome mentioned by Beaucamp, where Wicar's protégé Francesco Giangiacomo "maintained contact with his master's friends and enemies, gathering all of the city's rumours and keeping Wicar informed of them in timely fashion."[5]

At the turn of the eighteenth century, Wicar was one of the most prominent foreign artists working in Rome, where he cultivated a reputation as an excellent portraitist. During the French Revolution, he supported the revolutionary efforts of his fellow citizens in the Eternal City. A friend and frequent collaborator of David, he executed the drawing for the engraving *The Death of Marat* on his return to Paris in 1793. His association with David earned him the position of curator of antiquities at the Museum central des arts, and he was later sent to Italy by Napoleon Bonaparte to select works for shipment to France. Wicar chose to settle in Rome around 1800. He became a member of the Accademia di San Luca in 1805 and director of the Accademia di Belle Arte in Naples a year later. His large collection of Italian art is now held in the Musée des Beaux-Arts de Lille.

FIG 68 Jean-Baptiste Wicar, *Portrait of Piereff Romain*, Thomas Williams Fine Arts, London

FIG 69 Jean-Baptiste Wicar, *Portrait of Lorenzo Ré*, W.M. Brady & Co., Inc., New York

46

ATTRIBUTED TO FRANÇOIS-LOUIS-JOSEPH WATTEAU
Valenciennes 1758–1823 Lille
The Death of Montcalm c. 1783

FIG 70 Juste Chevillet, *The Death of the Marquis de Montcalm*, NGC

FIG 71 Benjamin West, *The Death of General Wolfe*, NGC

Brush and brown and grey wash
over black and red chalks,
heightened with white,
43.7 × 59.7 cm
Gift of W.A. Mather, Montreal,
1953
NO. 6172
PROVENANCE
L.G. Duke; Spink and Son,
London; W.A. Mather, Montreal.

Traditionally, this wash drawing was attributed to Louis-Joseph Watteau (called Watteau of Lille) because of the annotation at left under the border of the image by Juste Chevillet, published in 1783 (fig. 70). This attribution has, however, been revised by Laurier Lacroix, who believes the drawing to be the work of the elder Watteau's son François-Louis-Joseph.[1] Although the drawing, made over a preparatory sketch in red and black chalks, has nearly the same composition as the engraving except for being reversed, it is difficult to imagine that it was drawn in order to be engraved. Certain of its characteristics – the sometimes clumsy rendering, errors in the proportion of the bodies, and a depiction of natives that evokes the barbarians in the bas-reliefs of Roman Antiquity – encourage a cautious approach to that assumption.

In 1775, the new director general of buildings in Paris, the Count d'Angiviller, undertook to give a new direction to the development of French history painting, allowing modern history a place. The engraving by Chevillet and the drawing by Watteau are in that new spirit: they illustrate an episode in the Seven Years' War, the death of the Marquis Louis-Joseph de Montcalm on 13 September 1759, during the battle of the Plains of Abraham at Quebec City. The illustration of the French general dead on the battlefield, presented as a model of virtue, does not correspond to the known facts. Contrary to the annotation on the engraving, according to which Montcalm died in battle, the general was carried to the surgeon's residence and died there. He was buried the next day beneath the chapel of the Ursuline convent.[2]

It is important to note that this drawing and the corresponding engraving bear certain similarities to the composition of Benjamin West's painting *The Death of General Wolfe*, 1770 (fig. 71), which was known through William Woollett's widely disseminated engraving of 1776. The National Gallery of Canada also holds the preparatory drawing for West's painting, which dates to about 1769.

47
ANNE-LOUIS GIRODET DE ROUCY-TRIOSON
Montargis 1767–1824 Paris
The Death of Atala c. 1806–07

Pen and brown ink over graphite,
32.8 × 42.5 cm
PURCHASED 1973
NO. 17288
WATERMARK
In the centre, a crescent moon
crossed by two horizontal lines
PROVENANCE
Galerie du Fleuve, Paris.

FIG 72 Anne-Louis Girodet de Roucy-Trioson,
The Funeral of Atala, Musée du Louvre, Département
des peintures, Paris

This drawing by Anne-Louis Girodet de Roucy-Trioson is one of the initial compositional sketches for the painting *The Funeral of Atala* (fig. 72) in the Louvre, which Girodet submitted to the 1808 Salon. The artist was inspired by François René de Chateaubriand's short novel published in 1801, *Atala ou les amours de deux Sauvages dans le désert* ("Atala, or the loves of two savages in the wilderness"), a veritable manifesto in favour of the renewal of Christianity under the Bonapartist regime. Her friendship with the writer, and their shared political views, had a decisive influence on Girodet, as did the proliferation of an imagery of primitive man – and of Atala in particular – in the New World. This trend flourished throughout the nineteenth century in the wake of the success of Chateaubriand's novella and had its source in a vein of exoticism cultivated by a number of artists of the Romantic movement.[1]

Set in the forests of Louisiana in the seventeenth century, the love story has as its protagonists Atala – a young woman of mixed blood, illegitimate daughter of a Spanish father and a devout indigenous mother who had converted to Christianity – and the young Natchez Indian Chactas. Despite her promise to her mother to remain chaste and unmarried, Atala is on the point of giving in to her desire when she and her lover are discovered by Father Aubry, a French missionary, who offers them hospitality. Consumed by feelings of guilt, Atala takes her own life by swallowing a deadly poison. In the painting, Girodet depicts the moment following the discovery of Atala's inert body in the missionary's cave. Below a cross silhouetted against the horizon, amid a luxuriant forest, Atala lies cradled by the hands of the Franciscan missionary while her weeping lover clasps her legs.

Marked by an inspired dynamism and graphic verve, the Ottawa sketch differs considerably from another study in black chalk heightened with white (fig. 73) that offers a nearly definitive solution for the painting.[2] According to Hugh Honour, the Ottawa drawing illustrates the specific moment when Chactas promises Atala to convert to Christianity, and Father Aubry raises his arm and exclaims, "It is time to call upon God here."[3] From an profusion of repetitive lines, a dominant composition emerges. As McAllister Johnson has aptly pointed out, the sketch shows traces in graphite, indicating figure placement, in which the positioning of the lover is reversed, suggesting that Girodet may have decided in midstream to depict a different episode of the story.[4]

FIG 73 Anne-Louis Girodet de Roucy-Trioson, *Study for "The Funeral of Atala,"* Musée du Louvre, Cabinet des dessins, Paris

48

Jean Auguste Dominique Ingres
Montauban 1780–1867 Paris

Augustus, Octavia, and Livia Listening to Virgil Reading the "Aeneid"
("Tu Marcellus eris...") c. 1812–19

Graphite, laid on card,
39.9 × 32.3 cm
PURCHASED 1973
NO. 17134
WATERMARK
Partial, *VANDERLEY*
INSCRIPTION
Lower right, in graphite, *Ing*
PROVENANCE
Ingres sale, 1867 (L.1477); Émile
Bernard; Joseph Rignault, 1874
(L.2218); Jaccottet collection;
private collection, Zurich, starting
in the 1930s; Galerie Fritz et Peter
Nathan.

This refined and sensitive drawing (with the grid applied to it clearly visible) is one of a hundred or so works, including drawings,[1] paintings, and engravings, executed between 1812 and 1832 on the theme of Virgil reading the *Aeneid*.[2] Jean Auguste Dominique Ingres illustrates the moment when Octavia faints in the arms of her brother Augustus upon hearing Virgil recite *"Tu Marcellus eris,"* a passage from Book VI. Anchises' sombre "foretelling" of the death of her son Marcellus has aroused tragic memories. The empress Livia, responsible for the young man's demise, feigns concern about Octavia, while Augustus, with a gesture, commands Virgil to stop reading.

In this composition, as in the oldest known drawing on the theme, dated about 1812 and now in the Musée Ingres in Montauban, Patricia Condon has

FIG 74 Jean Auguste Dominique Ingres, *Augustus Listening to a Reading of the "Aeneid,"* Royal Museums for Art and History, Brussels

FIG 75 Jean Auguste Dominique Ingres, *Augustus Listening to a Reading of the "Aeneid,"* Fogg Art Museum, Harvard University Art Museums, Gift of Grenville L. Winthrop, class of 1886

detected a spirit similar to a Mannerist Descent from the Cross.[3] The same group of figures can be seen in the identical theme painting of around 1819, in Brussels (fig. 74), for which there are two studies on brown paper in graphite heightened with white in the Fogg Art Museum, Cambridge (fig. 75).[4] By 1812, Ingres had already painted a canvas on this subject, commissioned by General Miollis, which the artist bought back about 1835 and which shows signs of repainting; it is now in the Musée des Augustins, Toulouse.[5]

Condon has also demonstrated how difficult it is to date the works on this subject because of Ingres's habit of re-using the same subject many times and retouching old compositions, or asking his students to do so.[6] Given these circumstances, the chronology of his oeuvre is difficult to establish. It has been possible, nevertheless, to situate the Ottawa drawing in the early stages of establishing the layout of this subject. The most finished version of the theme is found in the engraving by Charles-Simon Pradier retouched by Ingres in 1832, which has an overall structure reminiscent of the painting in Toulouse.[7] In 1864, Ingres would use the same composition again, painting directly on Pradier's engraving.

49

THÉODORE GÉRICAULT
Rouen 1791–1824 Paris

Oenone and a Nymph VERSO: *Female Nude* c. 1816

Pen and brown ink over graphite with brown wash on buff wove paper, 20.6 × 12.6 cm
PURCHASED with the assistance of a contribution from Guy Wildenstein, New York, 2002
NO. 41034 r/v
PROVENANCE
Aimé-Charles-Horace His de la Salle (L. 1332), Paris; Sir Robert Ludwig Mond (L. suppl. 2813a), London; private collection until 1982 (sale, Sotheby Parke Bernet and Co., London, 16–17 June 1982, no. 565); Wildenstein and Co., New York.

This sheet is one of a series of studies for *Dying Paris Rejected by Oenone* done by Théodore Géricault at the École des Beaux-Arts in 1816, in preparation for the Prix de Rome competition.[1] Though they did not lead to the grand prize, which went to Antoine-Jean-Baptiste Thomas,[2] these studies announced the "antique manner"[3] that came to the fore during Géricault's stay in Italy (1816–17). Undertaken at his own expense, this trip saw him develop a distinctively fluid drawing style in strongly sensual works evocative of Italian Mannerism in both theme and graphic treatment.

The tale of Oenone and Paris is drawn from Homer's epic poem *The Iliad*. Oenone, a water nymph, is married to Paris, who abandons her to abduct the beautiful Helen with the help of Aphrodite. Gifted with prophetic sight, Oenone tries in vain to dissuade him, finally promising to use her healing powers if he is injured. But when Paris is shot by a poisoned arrow and begs her help, wounded pride and jealousy cause her to refuse. Her remorse comes too late: finding Paris dead, she takes her own life.

Géricault's free interpretation of the Homeric episode recalls the scene of Hector's funeral that adorns a sarcophagus in the Louvre. Indeed, a page from the Zoubaloff sketchbook reveals that the artist was familiar with this frieze (fig. 76).[4] As noted by Bazin, Géricault generally made both right-facing and left-facing sketches of his compositions.[5] The movement in the Ottawa sheet is directed towards the right, as it is in related sheets held in Bayonne (fig. 77), Dijon, Rouen, and Munich.

In the Ottawa drawing, Oenone, accompanied by one of her attendants, turns away from the entreating Paris. The detail on the recto shows the central figure draped in a diaphanous veil, hiding her eyes with her hand; in the background is a nymph depicted in a near-translucent manner. The drama expressed by the subject's pose is heightened by the intensity of the exceptionally spirited lines. The female nude on the verso, comparable to an academic figure, is notable for a finished, static appearance rendered in thick, firm lines.[6] Although the two sides of the sheet are graphically different, they are part of the same research, done in a short period of time, in which the female nude was executed before *Oenone and a Nymph*, according to Eitner.[7] Ultimately, *Oenone and a Nymph* reveals the young Géricault's classical influences, combined with the formal vigour and intensity of feeling that characterize a particular conception of Romanticism.

RECTO   VERSO

FIG 76 Théodore Géricault, *Page 36
verso of the Zoubaloff Sketchbook*, Musée
du Louvre, Cabinet des dessins,
Paris

FIG 77 Théodore Géricault, *Paris
Entreating Oenone*, Musée Bonnat,
Bayonne

50

FERDINAND-VICTOR-EUGÈNE DELACROIX

Charenton-Saint-Maurice 1798–1863 Paris

The Barque of Dante c. 1820

FIG 78 Eugène Delacroix, *The Barque of Dante*, Musée du Louvre, Département des peintures, Paris

Pen and brown ink with brown
wash and touches of grey wash
over graphite, 31 × 39.6 cm
Bequest of Ruth L. Massey Tovell,
Toronto, 1961
NO. 9729
PROVENANCE
Jenny Le Guillou (Delacroix's
governess); André Scholler, Paris;
Dr. H.M. Tovell, 1930; Ruth L.
Massey Tovell, Toronto.

Of all the sketches Ferdinand-Victor-Eugène Delacroix made for his painting *The Barque of Dante* of 1822 (fig. 78), in the Louvre, the sheet in Ottawa is the closest to the finished work the artist showed at his first Salon in 1822. On the basis of correspondence between Delacroix and his sister dated 11 March 1822, Lee Johnson associates this composition with the one drawn by the young artist during his stay in the forest of Boixe en Charente in September and early October of 1820, while he was suffering from a fever.[1] Although the attribution of some preliminary drawings remains hypothetical, Johnson believes this drawing comes from the very beginning of the development phase for the composition.[2]

As early as 1819, Delacroix was translating passages from *The Divine Comedy*,[3] the poem in which Dante recounts his imaginary voyage to Hell, Purgatory, and Paradise. The painter was particularly struck by a passage from the *Inferno* (Canto VIII), in which Virgil and Dante, in a boat steered by the ferryman Phlegias, cross the waters of the lake surrounding the walls of the City of Dis, the sixth circle of Hell. Delacroix chooses to represent the climactic moment of the psychological drama, when the damned try to cling to the boat. Trapp and Rubin point out how much the Ottawa drawing focuses on the figures of Dante and Virgil, captured in a theatrical pose.[4] Depicted in lighter tones, they dominate the pyramidal composition, while Phlegias blends into the background. Note also how the strongly applied monochromatic brown wash adds to the pathos of the scene.

In the painting, Delacroix accords greater importance to the boat, as it is assailed on all sides by the damned. The finished work shows clearly the influence of Rubens and Michelangelo in the musculature of the bodies and the rendering of draperies, and also of Géricault, whose *Raft of the Medusa* of 1819, in the Louvre, inspired the young Delacroix.[5] A comparable theme had been treated in 1807 by the English artist John Flaxman in an engraving based on Canto III of the *Inferno*, in which Charon, in his boat on the river Acheron, ferries the souls to the far shore.[6]

51
FERDINAND-VICTOR-EUGÈNE DELACROIX
Charenton-Saint-Maurice 1798–1863 Paris
Christ on the Cross c. 1853–56

FIG 79 Eugène Delacroix,
Crucifixion, The National Gallery,
London

FIG 80 Eugène Delacroix, *Christ on
the Cross*, NGC

This pastel is one of the many Crucifixion scenes painted or drawn by Ferdinand-Victor-Eugène Delacroix, who repeatedly explored this theme beginning in the 1830s. In official commissions and church decorations, he initially approached religious painting as "a veritable campaign to reconquer public opinion."[1] After 1850, his interest in religious subjects became a spiritual quest, manifested as much in his chosen themes – mainly from the New Testament – as in their treatment. Among his best-known Crucifixions, the one shown at the 1835 Salon was purchased by the French government and presented as a gift to the City of Vannes for the Saint-Patern church. For the 1846 and 1853 Salons,[2] he returned to the same motif. All of these variations on a single theme were inspired by the paintings *Christ on the Cross between the Two Thieves* and a Crucifixion known as the *Coup de lance* by Rubens, whose influence on Delacroix was decisive.[3]

In its general approach the Ottawa sheet relates to the 1853 painting, which is in the National Gallery in London (fig. 79). However, the drawing has a mystical dimension not found in the painted work; Christ is portrayed alone, in a dark and barren landscape, a serpent at his feet. This attribute represents Evil vanquished by Christ's piety, a symbol of redemption. The collection in Ottawa also contains a preliminary graphite drawing for the pastel, which features the same desolate view (fig. 80). Despite a variation in the position of the feet, the background landscape, the posture of Christ's body, and the presence of the serpent at the foot of the cross establish a certain connection between the two drawings.[4]

Pastel on grey-blue paper,
24.7 × 16.5 cm
PURCHASED 1968
NO. 15733
INSCRIPTION
At lower left, *Eug. delacroix*
PROVENANCE
Adolphe Beugniet, Paris;
M. Mallet, Paris; Mme Philippe
Vernes, Paris, 1930–63 (?); Bernard
Laurenceau, Paris; Marianne
Feilchenfeldt, Zurich, 1968.

52

ALEXANDRE-GABRIEL DECAMPS
Paris 1803–1860 Fontainebleau
A Cowherd and His Cattle Crossing a Stream in Stormy Weather c. 1830–40

Charcoal with pastel and white
chalk on brown wove paper, laid
down on wove paper, 23.3 × 30 cm
PURCHASED 1912
NO. 348
PROVENANCE
Cottier and Co. Gallery, New York.

In this stormy landscape, Alexandre-Gabriel Decamps creates an astonishing effect through his technique. By amalgamating or overlaying charcoal and pastels in light colours – yellow, pink, and white – he gives the scene an intensely atmospheric quality. On the basis of this visual experience, this subtle play of light and dark tonal values, Decamps' work can be linked with Romanticism, although he would never accept that label.[1] From his numerous voyages, which took him from Europe to Asia Minor, the artist brought back exotic subjects and picturesque scenes, as well as a large number of landscapes inspired by the places he visited. Categorized as an Orientalist painter, Decamps initially submitted two works to the 1827 Salon, *Soldier of a Vizier's Guard* and *Hunting Lapwings*. His subsequent Salon participation would be sporadic.

Throughout his career, Decamps often worked on several projects at the same

FIG 81 Alexandre-Gabriel Decamps, *A Goatherd of the Abruzzi*, NGC

time, so it is hard to situate this drawing in his oeuvre.[2] It is not difficult, however, to relate the morphology of this landscape to that of *The Defeat of the Cimbri*, 1833, in the Louvre, for which two drawings exist, one at the Musée Bonnat, Bayonne.[3] Moreover, the National Gallery of Canada has a painting in its collection, *A Goatherd of the Abruzzi*, 1845 (fig. 81),[4] in which the protagonist is wearing a hat of a conical shape that is repeated in the silhouette of the cowherd in this drawing.

53

THOMAS COUTURE
Senlis 1815–1879 Villiers-le-Bel

Study for "Horace and Lydia" VERSO: *Hindquarters of an Animal* c. 1843

RECTO

VERSO

FIG 82 Thomas Couture, *Horace and Lydia*, The Wallace Collection, London

Black chalk, heightened with white chalk on grey-blue laid paper, 13.6 × 16 cm
PURCHASED 1974
NO. 17910
INSCRIPTION
In the lower-left quadrant, *T. C*
PROVENANCE
Sale, Hôtel Drouot, Paris, 25 June 1973, no. 66; Galerie du Fleuve, Paris.

This drawing by Thomas Couture may be compared with the painting *Horace and Lydia*, 1843 (fig. 82), in the Wallace Collection,[1] which Boime correctly saw as a precursor of the artist's masterpiece, *Romans of the Decadence*, now in the Musée d'Orsay, Paris,[2] Couture's entry in the Salon of 1847. The Venetian influences on the painter, in his style and choice of Bacchic themes, can be seen in the latter composition and in all works created after 1843.[3] Despite the impression of preciosity evoked by its small size, the Ottawa sheet has its source in a similar spirit. Particularly noteworthy is the strong sensuality of the rendering, resulting from a subtle use of black and white chalks on blue paper, traditionally associated with the drawings of several Venetian artists of the Renaissance. Couture used the same technique and support as well as a black outline on other occasions, as in the study for his *Little Pastry Cook* at the Musée des Beaux-Arts in Algiers.[4]

In developing the composition of *Horace and Lydia*, Couture freely drew inspiration from one of Horace's poems (Odes I, 36–38), taking specific characteristics of the servant, in the background, and of Lydia, the Roman courtesan embracing Horace. The poet is impassive, holding out his cup so the slave can fill it with wine. Horace (65–8 B.C.) condemned avarice, ambition, and passion, and was in favour of prostitution so that men could maintain their emotional purity. An Epicurean, he hailed the liberating virtue of wine. He believed in the pleasures of the senses, without, however, renouncing morality.[5] Here, for the first time in his career as a painter, the young Couture adopts a theme from Antiquity to criticize, and satirize, contemporary society.[6]

54
JEAN-LÉON GÉRÔME
Vesoul 1824–1904 Paris
Aswan: Study for "Donkey Driver in Cairo" 1856

Black chalk on wove paper,
26.4 × 16.1 cm
PURCHASED 1977
NO. 18877
INSCRIPTIONS
At lower left, *dessin de JL Gerome*; in
the lower-right quadrant, *Assouan*
PROVENANCE
Aimé Morot (Gérôme's son-in-
law); Galerie de Bayser, Paris, 1977,
no. 17; Hazlitt, Gooden and Fox
Ltd., London.

Of an almost photographic clarity, this study of a young Arab was included in an album containing a number of drawings that evoke the first voyage of Jean-Léon Gérôme to Egypt, in 1856–57, in the company of Frédéric Masson and Émile Augier. While some of these drawings illustrate landscapes, most testify to the young artist's marked interest in the inhabitants of the places he visited. In most cases, these portraits bear annotations – sometimes in French and Arabic – about the identity and origin of the subject. A fine, precise line emphasizes the outlines and the folds of fabric, while the shadows are fashioned from short, regular strokes of hatching.

Some of these drawings were preparatory studies for paintings, including this portrait, annotated *Assouan*,[1] which later served as the basis for *Donkey Driver in Cairo*, 1860, a painting that has disappeared.[2] Attesting its success, the work was reproduced by Goupil & Co. in 1861,[3] and Frédéric-Auguste Laguillermie made an etching of the same image in about 1880 (fig. 83) for an album of works by different artists.[4] Note that the theme of the donkey driver and his mount recurs on a number of occasions in Gérôme's paintings.[5] After an apprenticeship with Paul Delaroche, the painter glimpsed the Orient for the first time in 1844 when he studied briefly with Charles Gleyre, one of the first French artists to visit Egypt and to be inspired by it in his work.[6]

FIG 83 Frédéric-Auguste
Laguillermie, *Donkey Driver in Cairo*,
Bibliothèque nationale, Paris

The 19th Century

New Perspectives

55

GUSTAVE COURBET

Ornans 1819–1877 La Tour-de-Peilz

The Black Arm 1856

Black pencil on wove paper,
47.3 × 51.6 cm
PURCHASED 1978
NO. 23146
INSCRIPTION
At lower right, *G. C.*
PROVENANCE
Jules Champfleury, Paris; Galerie
Durand-Ruel, Paris; Wildenstein
and Co., New York; private
collection, New York; John and
Paul Herring and Co., New York.

This drawing is distinguished by its literary subject, which at first glance seems unusual in the oeuvre of Gustave Courbet. The founder of Realism drew *The Black Arm* to publicize Fernand Desnoyers' pantomime, written in verse and premiered by the actor Paul Legrand on 8 February 1856, at the Théâtre des Folies-Nouvelles. Reproduced as a poster, the drawing served as a model for a wood engraving used to decorate the frontispiece of a booklet describing the pantomime that was published by the Librairie théâtrale.[1] Following the lead of Clark, Humbert and Stuffmann emphasized that Courbet's collaboration in this enterprise was primarily the result of his friendship with Jules Champfleury[2] and his connections with members of literary circles that included Desnoyers, who used to visit the painter's Paris studio at 32 rue Hautefeuille. The Ottawa sheet can be considered one of the best examples of the meeting of different artistic domains – theatre, literature, drawing, and engraving – all of which contributed to the emergence of the Realist movement. In his analysis of Champfleury's interest in pantomime, Clark has implied that this genre, with its tendency toward parody, its simplicity, and an audience consisting of children and ordinary people, shared the same spirit.[3]

In this large drawing, with its especially dramatic pictorial effect, Courbet depends on contrasts in tonal value for his effects, saturating his drawing with black and leaving as the reserve only the white figure of Pierrot. This graphic process helps accentuate the tragi-comic nature of the episode. In love with Nini, Pierrot engages in a rivalry with the Moor Scapin, whom the beautiful Nini prefers. During a scuffle, Pierrot rips off Scapin's arm and has one of his own torn off; the evil black arm of Scapin becomes Pierrot's own – it is reattached by Doctor Roidamos – and causes him many problems. Meanwhile, his honest white arm tries to counter the evil actions of the black arm. Pierrot's misfortunes end when he is arrested for debauchery, and loses the noxious limb. On the left side of the image, the black arm, outstretched and threatening, seems to rise out of the earth; while on the right, at the feet of the terrified Pierrot, is the sack of gold stolen by Scapin from Pierrot's father, Cassandre. At last, the good doctor helps Pierrot to grow a new white arm, and our hero marries Chimène, the daughter of the rich Polichinelle.

According to Cazort, the drawing illustrates the moment after the departure of Nini – who has dropped the purse – when Pierrot's struggle against evil has already begun.[4] Note that French pantomime in the nineteenth century reworked and adapted the traditional characters of the Italian commedia dell'arte from which it drew its inspiration.

56

GUSTAVE MOREAU

Paris 1826–1898 Paris

Hesiod and the Muse 1858

Pen and brown ink, black chalk and
brown wash, heightened with
opaque white and watercolour, on
heavy cream wove paper,
37.6 × 29 cm
PURCHASED 1966
NO. 15213
INSCRIPTIONS
At bottom left, GM. [superimposed]
Gustave Moreau. Rome. 1858.
PROVENANCE
M. Brame, Paris; Antoine-François
Marmontel (1816–1898), Paris;
Marmontel sale, Hôtel Drouot,
Paris, 25–26 January 1883, lot 210;
Marmontel estate sale, Hôtel
Drouot, Paris, 28–29 March 1898,
lot 173; Guillaume Mallet; Galerie
Stephen Higgons, Paris.

FIG 84 Gustave Moreau, *Hesiod and the Muse*, Musée d'Orsay, Paris

FIG 85 Gustave Moreau, *Hesiod and the Muse*, Fogg Art Museum, Harvard University Art Museums, Anonymous loan

FIG 86 Gustave Moreau, *Study for an antique bas-relief, Sleeping Endymion*, Musée Gustave-Moreau, Paris

This monochrome drawing of great refinement demonstrates graphic prowess worthy of Italian Mannerism, with pen, wash, black chalk, and watercolour blending to create a hazy atmospheric effect. The subtle relief is marked by delicate heightening in opaque white, applied with a brush, and by fine lines drawn with the pen, sometimes cross-hatched. For the shadows, the artist skilfully combines black chalk and fine hatchings in pen and brown ink. *Hesiod and the Muse* dates from Gustave Moreau's stay in Italy in 1857–59, from which he brought back drawings primarily after the masters of the Renaissance and monuments of Antiquity. Four other studies on the same themes, dating from 1857, were done prior to the example in Ottawa;[1] this drawing was shown in the 1866 Salon, but the painted version, which has a completely different feeling, would not be created until 1891 (fig. 84).

According to Mathieu, this drawing and another large sheet in the Fogg collection (fig. 85) are among the only original compositions done by Moreau in Italy; they have the virtue of showing the development of his style out of a classicism that here still seems to be somewhat affected.[2] For example, the languid pose of the sleeping Hesiod shows the influence of the figure of Endymion in a bas-relief in the Capitoline Museum in Rome, of which the young artist made a copy that is today in the Musée Gustave-Moreau (fig. 86).[3]

The choice of subject derives from the young artist's admiration of Eugène Delacroix, who, around 1842, had done the decoration for the cupola devoted to poetry in the library of the Palais Bourbon. Delacroix had painted the Muse hovering over the sleeping Hesiod, inspiring him with poetry.[4] Taken from the *Theogony*, the myth relates that the Muses, daughters of Zeus, instilled the gift of the arts in the shepherd Hesiod (700 B.C.) while he tended his sheep at the foot of Mount Helicon. The shepherd chose Calliope, Muse of epic poetry, as chief among her sisters. Moreau depicts Calliope inspiring the slumbering Hesiod by breathing on his face. In his account of the 1866 Salon, Ernest Chesneau described the drawing eloquently:

The shepherd, young and handsome, wearing a Phrygian bonnet over his long, floating hair, is listening, eyes shut in concentration, to the inspired message whispered to him by the Muse, who has descended from Olympus on her great wings, ethereal, suspended like a weightless cloud, gently brushing the poet's forehead with her fingers and her sweet breath.[5]

57

PIERRE CÉCIL PUVIS DE CHAVANNES

Lyon 1824–1898 Paris

The Toilette c. 1883

Black chalk, heightened with white
chalk on tracing paper, laid down
on card, 29.9 × 26.1 cm (irreg.)

PURCHASED 1983

NO. 28269

INSCRIPTION

At upper right, *à mon ami Bouillon* /
Puvis

PROVENANCE

Bouillon (?); Jacques Dubourg,
Paris; sale, Hôtel Drouot, Paris,
10 December 1981, no. 81 (?); Margo
Pollins Schab, New York.

Of the large number of studies by Pierre Cécil Puvis de Chavannes for his
painting *Young Woman at Her Toilette*, 1883 (fig. 87), the drawing in Ottawa
appears to be the closest to the final version, not only because it contains all the
elements of the final composition, but also because of its emphatic rendering with
strong lines. Various authors have pointed out the difficulty in establishing a
straightforward chronology for the works on this theme, but the drawing *Seated
Woman* (fig. 88) in the Petit Palais collection offers a simplified version of the Ottawa
sheet. While the servant-woman in the background is not present, the young
woman holding a mirror – which would be exchanged for a bouquet of flowers in

FIG 88 Puvis de Chavannes, *Seated Woman, Study for "Young Woman at Her Toilette,"* Petit Palais, Paris

FIG 87 Puvis de Chavannes, *Young Woman at Her Toilette*, Musée d'Orsay, Paris

the painting – and the dish of fruit are clearly visible. Like Brown Price, most authors also concur in assuming a connection with the small painting on millboard in the National Gallery in London, *The Toilette*, c. 1877–83.[1] In appearance trivial, the subject of a young woman at her ablutions, unclothed and passive, becomes, in the hands of Puvis de Chavannes, an updated representation of Venus, the goddess of love, or even the biblical figure Esther. Brown Price also sees a link with Degas' pastel *A Woman Having Her Hair Combed*, 1886–88, at the Metropolitan Museum of Art.[2]

More than a decade after showing his painting at the *Exposition nationale des beaux-arts*, Puvis de Chavannes again used the Ottawa composition for a photolithograph entitled *La toilette*, published in 1895 in the newspaper *L'Épreuve* with four other prints of his old compositions.[3] Only when it was acquired in 1983 was this sheet identified by Douglas Druick as the drawing – formerly thought to be lost – that was used as the model for the print.[4] Toward the end of his life, Puvis de Chavannes would re-use the same composition in a mythological version, *The Toilette of Thetis*, 1896, in the Art Institute of Chicago,[5] before painting a *Mary Magdalene*, 1897 (fig. 89), with a landscape as background, which betrays its source despite its almost decorative simplicity.[6]

FIG 89 Puvis de Chavannes, *Mary Magdalene*, Szépmüvészeti Múzeum, Budapest

58
GUSTAVE CHRISTOPHE PAUL DORÉ
Strasbourg 1832–1883 Paris

"For the rare and radiant maiden whom the angels name Lenore — Nameless here for evermore!"
Illustration for Edgar Allan Poe's Poem "The Raven" 1882–83

Pen and brown ink with grey wash
over graphite, on wove paper,
52.5 × 35.5 cm
PURCHASED 1966
NO. 14935
INSCRIPTION
At lower right, signed, *G Doré*
PROVENANCE
Berry-Hill Galleries, New York.

FIG 90 After Gustave Doré,
Illustration for "The Raven,"
Bibliothèque nationale, Paris

Gustave Doré did this drawing for the fifth plate (fig. 90) in a series of twenty-six wood engravings, including a frontispiece, a half-title, and twenty-four plates,[1] intended to illustrate an edition of Edgar Allan Poe's poem *The Raven*, first published in 1845. The verses express the poet's sadness at the inescapable demise of his young wife, Virginia, represented in the poem in the guise of Lenore,[2] who would succumb to tuberculosis in 1847. The illustration of this elegiac poem was, in fact, Doré's last work, published in England shortly after his death.

The artist employs a symbolic repertory vaguely reminiscent of what he used for his interpretations of *The Divine Comedy* and the Bible in 1866. He succeeds in creating evocative images in which the real and the imaginary intermingle. Ségolène Le Men notes that the Ottawa drawing, with its cortege of angels, brings to mind an iconography appropriate to illustrate the episode of Jacob's dream in the Bible,[3] for example. This sheet refers specifically to the passage at the end of the second stanza in which the poet recalls his beloved Lenore; in the drawing, angels, against a glowing background, are bearing her away to heaven:

> — *vainly I had sought to borrow*
> *From my books surcease of sorrow — sorrow for the lost Lenore —*
> *For the rare and radiant maiden whom the angels name Lenore —*
> *Nameless here for evermore!*[4]

59
ODILON REDON
Bordeaux 1840–1916 Paris
The Raven 1882

Charcoal, 39.9 × 27.9 cm
PURCHASED 1965
NO. 14847
INSCRIPTION
At lower right, signed, *Od. R.*
PROVENANCE
Ambroise Vollard, Paris; Stephen
Higgons, Paris.

This drawing by Odilon Redon was re-used as a lithograph to decorate the cover of a collection of stories by Edgar Allan Poe translated into French by Émile Hennequin and published in 1882 under the title of *Contes grotesques* (Ollendorff, Paris).[1] Originally, *The Raven* was supposed to be the frontispiece of the work, but when the book appeared, Redon discovered to his dismay that his work had been disfigured by type.[2] To make things worse, the drawing Redon made for Hennequin had nothing to do with the title of the work, which did not even include the poem. This blunder by the publisher did not lessen the friendship Redon felt for Hennequin, who had introduced him to Poe's writing in the 1870s.

Roseline Bacou has found another sheet in the Musée des Beaux-Arts de Bordeaux which depicts a young woman with a raven at her feet.[3] In 1882, Redon also did a series of seven lithographs, including a frontispiece, in honour of Poe.[4] Before Redon, other artists, among them Doré (see cat. 58) and Manet had produced illustrations to accompany the poem in its original English version or the 1875 French translation by Mallarmé.[5]

The coarse and in some respects banal character of this drawing is surprising. Bacou suggests that it (in contrast to the sheet in the Louvre) may be a literal illustration rather than an evocation of Poe's poem.[6] Of an intense black, almost schematic in design, the large bird perched on the sill of an open window has an equivalent, if not its source, in the illustration for a frontispiece engraved by Linley Sambourne for *The Poems of Edgar Allan Poe*, published in London in 1881.[7]

60

ODILON REDON

Bordeaux 1840–1916 Paris

The Poet and Pegasus (Captive Pegasus) c. 1891–98

Charcoal on wove paper,
48.2 × 37.7 cm

PURCHASED 1965

NO. 14846

INSCRIPTION

At lower right, signed in purple
ink, *Od. R.*

PROVENANCE

Madame Redon; Ambroise Vollard,
Paris, c. 1900; Stephen Higgons,
Paris.

That the subject of Pegasus occupied Odilon Redon's imagination for several years is attested by this large sheet, along with many other drawings, paintings, and engravings.[1] Mesley proposes dating this drawing after the lithograph entitled *Captive Pegasus*, 1889 (fig. 91), while linking it to another of 1898, *Pilgrim of the Sublunary World*. Redon continued exploring the theme until about 1898, when he created *Man on Pegasus, or The Poet and Pegasus*.[2]

In Greek mythology, the winged horse Pegasus is born of the blood of Medusa after Perseus cuts off her head. While drinking at the spring of Peirene, Pegasus is captured by Bellerophon, who uses him to slay the Chimera. Once he has accomplished his mission with the aid of the winged steed, Bellerophon wants to ascend Mount Olympus and join the gods, but Zeus, angered at his presumption, causes Pegasus to throw him off. Pegasus, now free, makes his way to his place in the heavens.

In this drawing, Pegasus, symbol of poetic inspiration, bears Bellerophon on his back, who is holding a bridle made of laurel leaves, standing for artistic accomplishment and immortality. The horse evokes even more grandeur and nobility in that he occupies most of the sheet, relegating the figure of his rider to secondary importance. The lithograph *Captive Pegasus*, similar in spirit, would inspire Redon's friend, the collector André Mellario,[3] to write a sonnet entitled *La grande capture*[4] in 1893.

The composition of the Ottawa drawing provides an excellent example of the virtuosity with which Redon handles his "blacks" – the word the artist used to describe certain drawings, etchings, and lithographs executed between 1860 and 1895.[5] Redon would scratch, rub, and stump the unstable charcoal pigment to obtain an effect that evoked a fantastic world, with figures delineated only by a fine or even broken line. In this drawing, it is the materiality of the work as much as the iconography used that calls to mind poetry and the world of the imagination.

FIG 91 Odilon Redon, *Captive Pegasus*, NGC

61

Jean-Baptiste Camille Corot
Paris 1796–1875 Ville-d'Avray

The Bridge at Narni VERSO: *Two Landscape Studies* (not illustrated) c. 1826–27

FIG 92 Camille Corot, *The Bridge at Narni*, NGC

FIG 93 Camille Corot, *The Bridge at Narni*, Musée du Louvre, Département des peintures, Paris

Graphite on wove paper,
30.3 × 46.6 cm
PURCHASED 1963
NO. 9969
PROVENANCE
Corot sale (L. 461, stamped in red);
Calligaris collection, Lyon; Galerie
Feilchenfeldt, Zurich.

Jean-Baptiste Camille Corot made this drawing on his first trip to Italy, probably while he was staying in the neighbourhood of Narni in September 1826.[1] The
young artist was following in the footsteps of his teacher Michallon, who had visited the region to study the local landscape.[2] Apparently drawn from nature, the study
was then used for an oil painting that was completed in the studio and shown at the
1827 Salon, *The Bridge at Narni* (fig. 92); an oil sketch for the painting is found in the
Louvre (fig. 93). The bridge, built in the reign of the Emperor Augustus, crosses the
Nera, a river that runs through a deep gorge below the ancient town of Narni.

The drawing in Ottawa lays down the initial formal ideas for the canvas and
shows a more meticulous execution and a more distant viewpoint than the oil sketch
in the Louvre, which was probably used to work out the colours and light.[3] In contrast to the oil sketch, the drawing and the finished work do not include the
escarpment on the left. The painting in Ottawa, inspired by Nicolas Poussin and
Claude Lorrain, offers an example of integration of the traditional classical landscape and direct observation; the Ottawa sheet and two other drawings at the
Louvre are, moreover, the only examples that have come down to us of the earliest stages of development of the painting.[4] Compared with the final work, the
Ottawa drawing shows greater flexibility, particularly in the accentuated outlines
and the darker areas that suggest variations of light and shadow. The preliminary
composition allows more space to the watercourse in which the cattle are slaking
their thirst, which is not in the painting. Corot would re-use this element, in
reversed position, in his *Italian Landscape* of circa 1835, in the J. Paul Getty Museum,
Los Angeles.[5]

62

CHARLES-FRANÇOIS DAUBIGNY
Paris 1817–1878 Paris

Landscape with Figures and Animals in Windy Weather: Study for "Les Graves à Villerville" c. 1859

Surrounded by a pencilled line, this small landscape primarily draws its acute expressiveness from the gusts of wind suggested by the bending trees. Charles-François Daubigny treats this scene of bad weather with a jerky, sometimes double line, using to good effect the contrast between intermittent and regular hatching. Recognizable in this windblown landscape are the salt flats at Villerville, in the Calvados region of Normandy, which Daubigny painted on several occasions between 1858 and his death. From these stays in Normandy, the artist acquired a great familiarity with nature, which he depicted tirelessly, prefiguring the Impressionists in his ability to render effects of light.[1]

The drawing in Ottawa is specifically related to the painting shown at the 1859 Salon, *Les Graves à Villerville* (fig. 94), today in Marseille, with a copy in the Louvre.[2] All of the artist's views of this feature show the same geography and the identical arrangements of trees and animals, as well as the two figures seated in the foreground. The spontaneous aspect of the drawing and its small size suggest that the scene was drawn from nature. The addition of red chalk scumbling in the area representing the sky contributes to the intensity of the image.

FIG 94 Charles-François Daubigny, *Les Graves à Villerville*, Musée des Beaux-Arts, Marseille

Graphite and red chalk rubbing
on wove paper, 17.7 × 27.3 cm
PURCHASED 1912

NO. 351

INSCRIPTIONS
At lower left, under the border of
the image, signed, *Daubigny*; at lower
centre of the sheet, *D. Daubigny*

PROVENANCE
Daubigny sale, Paris, 6–11 May 1878
(L. 518, stamped in red); Cottier
and Co. Gallery, New York.

63

CAMILLE PISSARRO
Saint Thomas 1830–1903 Paris

Church and Farm at Éragny-sur-Epte c. 1894–95

FIG 95 Camille Pissarro, *Church and Farm at Éragny-sur-Epte*, NGC

FIG 96 Camille Pissarro, *The Church at Éragny*, The Metropolitan Museum of Art, New York, Harris Brisbane Dick Fund, 1948

FIG 97 Camille Pissarro, *Landscape at Éragny: Church and Farm*, Musée d'Orsay, Paris

Pen and brown ink with borders in graphite on beige wove paper; drawing: 15.9 × 25 cm; sheet: 20.1 × 26 cm

PURCHASED 1981

NO. 26618

INSCRIPTIONS

Recto, lower left, in pen and brown ink, *Église et la ferme d'Éragny-sur-Epte*; lower right, in pen and brown ink, *C. Pissarro*

PROVENANCE

Sir Edward Beddington-Behrens, from Zdenek Bruck (sale, Sotheby's, London, 1 July 1959, no. 2); sale, Berne, 15 June 1980, no. 1208; Galerie Kornfeld, Düsseldorf.

This view of Éragny-sur-Epte should be compared with two versions of an etching, one in black ink and one in colour (fig. 95) for which six different print states exist.[1] Surrounded by a pencilled line whose dimensions correspond within a few millimetres to the size of the print as it came off the plate, the image is formed of stiff, scribbled pen marks that resemble the effect produced by a burin scraping away varnish on an etching plate. The contrast between the areas containing varying amounts of drawing and the spaces purposely left as reserve creates a vibrantly luminous impression. Another drawing, of 1890, with the same composition in charcoal (fig. 96) shows the same countryside except for the human figures and the cattle,[2] but the treatment is much more perfunctory. All the drawn versions have a connection with a painting dated 1895, *Landscape at Éragny: Church and Farm* (fig. 97),[3] which shows a view from a higher elevation, however, with a different arrangement of trees and cattle.

Éragny is a small village in the Oise, north of Paris; the slender steeple of its church appears frequently in Pissarro's work. For some twenty years, starting in 1884, the artist depicted this rural area, its meadows, and inhabitants, and used his observations to experiment with light and other effects in his paintings. He carried out similar explorations in his prints, as well as in hundreds of drawings[4] and watercolours, which he collected in portfolios.[5]

64

PAUL CÉZANNE
Aix-en-Provence 1839–1906 Aix-en-Provence
Study of Trees VERSO: *Landscape with House and Trees* 1888–99

Graphite; verso, watercolour over
traces of graphite on wove paper,
47.2 × 31.5 cm
PURCHASED 1979
NO. 23532 r/v
PROVENANCE
Ambroise Vollard, Paris; Dr. Simon
Meller, Budapest and Munich; Paul
Cassirer, Amsterdam; Franz
Koenigs, Rotterdam; Mr. and Mrs.
van der Waals-Koenigs, Heemstede;
John and Paul Herring and Co.,
New York.

It is difficult to date this two-sided sheet with certainty; Paul Cézanne was not in the habit of signing or dating his works. According to various authors' observations, however, both sides were probably drawn during his mature phase but with an interval of several years between them.[1] During that period, 1888 to 1899, the Provençal artist began to earn recognition in the Parisian art world, notably in 1895 when the gallery owner Ambroise Vollard presented the first exhibition devoted to his work.

Comparing this sheet with other drawings by Cézanne, Mesley recognized in the watercolour a view from Jas de Bouffan, the artist's family residence,[2] but Cézanne's preoccupation with form meant that he was not particularly concerned with depicting a specific place. For him, the countryside was rather a subject for experimentation, in which every motif fit into a unified whole constructed of forms and surfaces.[3] Thus, on the verso of the sheet, the two sides of a slope evoke the roof of a house, while at the right, a narrow vertical strip left as reserve suggests the slender trunk of a tree. Attention is focused on the real subject of the work: the different intensities of the shadows, rendered by areas of watercolour shading from green to dark blue. The graphite line disappears, becoming merely suggestive if not superfluous.

The recto drawing – considered to be later – appears in certain respects more naturalistic, despite its simple, almost austere aspect. A broad path can be distinguished, bordered by trees whose twisted branches seem leafless. In contrast to the watercolour on the verso, in which flat areas of colour lend a two-dimensional character, here the placement of the trees in a slanting line is a visual strategy that the viewer interprets as perspective. There are also some areas delicately shaded with pencil which produce a contoured effect.

65

HILAIRE GERMAIN EDGAR DEGAS
Montargis 1834–1917 Paris
Alexander and Bucephalus c. 1859–61

Graphite, watercolour, and oil, on
tan laid paper, mounted on cream
wove paper, 51.4 × 38.2 cm
PURCHASED 1998
NO. 39657
PROVENANCE
Degas sale (L. 658, stamped in red);
artist's estate; Robert von Hirsch
(sale, Sotheby's, London, 27 June
1978, lot 816); S.M. Golestaneh,
London (sale, Sotheby's, London,
26 March 1986, no. 308); private
collection (sale, Sotheby's, London,
9 December 1997, lot 203).

A more developed version of this subject exists in the form of an unfinished painting now in the collection of the National Gallery of Art in Washington (fig. 98). This large sheet is one of Edgar Degas' first known works. The artist's notebooks dating from his stay in Italy (1856–59) contain the first indications of his formal and iconographic experiments in preparation for the painting *Alexander and Bucephalus*, which he began upon his return to Paris but abandoned in 1861. Among the score of such preparatory studies in graphite or ink in the notebooks are some that illustrate the landscape in which the scene would be set, while others are studies of draped figures or of Bucephalus viewed from different angles.[1] The young artist was attempting to renew the historical genre both thematically and stylistically, while tackling two other paintings whose subjects were equally unusual, *Jephthah's Daughter* and *Semiramis Building Babylon*.[2]

The application of oil over the watercolour hints at the ultimate purpose of this study: the final version was intended to be Degas' first submission to the Salon, but it was replaced by *Semiramis Building Babylon*. Similar in appearance to the faded colours of Italian Renaissance frescoes, the Ottawa sketch also shows the influence of Jean Auguste Dominique Ingres, Degas' teacher. Douglas Cooper was the first to note a connection with Ingres's *Triumph of Romulus over Acron*, in the École nationale supérieure des beaux-arts, Paris.[3] Theodore Reff points out that about 1860, Degas copied the draped figure of Apelles painted by Ingres in *The Apotheosis of Homer*, 1827 (location unknown).[4]

For this drawing, Degas was inspired by the passage from Plutarch's *Lives* that relates the episode from the youth of Alexander the Great in which, under the eyes of his father, King Philip of Macedon, Alexander meets the challenge of taming the horse Bucephalus, who is considered too wild to be ridden. Noticing that the horse shies away from his own shadow, the young man turns him to face the sun and thus succeeds in mounting him. Surprised at this accomplishment, King Philip spurs his son to seek a kingdom of his own. Bucephalus will become Alexander's faithful steed, accompanying him on his campaigns in Greece, Persia, Egypt, and lands farther east. The image of the youthful Alexander managing to tame the beast through his intelligence and perspicacity presages his future conquests. The subject is one rarely treated in painting: the use of it by Degas early in his career is interesting in that it suggests an analogy with the young artist's ambition to master his art.

FIG 98 Edgar Degas, *Alexander and Bucephalus*, National Gallery of Art, Washington, D.C., Bequest of Lore Heinemann in memory of her husband, Dr. Rudolf J. Heinemann

66

Henri de Toulouse-Lautrec

Albi 1864–1901 Château de Malromé, Gironde

Amédée Tapié de Céleyran 1882

Charcoal, 63.2 × 47.3 cm
Gift of Mrs. Samuel Bronfman,
O.B.E., Westmount, Quebec, 1973,
in memory of her late husband
Samuel Bronfman, C.C., LL.D.
NO. 17587
WATERMARK
MICHALLET
PROVENANCE
Artist's stamp (L. 1338); Mrs.
Samuel Bronfman, O.B.E.

Drawn in the summer of 1882, this full-length portrait of Amédée Tapié de Céleyran is one of Henri de Toulouse-Lautrec's youthful works, along with dozens of other portraits of family members.[1] Including this sheet, the National Gallery of Canada holds seven such works, all large, from the collection of Mrs. Samuel Bronfman: *Charles de Toulouse-Lautrec* (no. 17588), *The Artist's Mother, Countess Adèle de Toulouse-Lautrec* (no. 17589), two portraits of *Raoul Tapié de Céleyran* (nos. 17590 and 17591), and portraits of the artist's grandmothers, *Gabrielle de Toulouse-Lautrec* (no. 17592) and *Louise Tapié de Céleyran* (no. 17593).

This full-length depiction, with its frontal view, is something of an exception among the family portraits; the others in the series are invariably busts. The features of Uncle Amédée — Toulouse-Lautrec's mother's brother, with whom he kept up an extended correspondence — are also immortalized in one of his more traditional effigy busts, which were usually signed *Monfa* and date to 1882 (fig. 99).[2]

A short stay of barely three months in the studio of Léon Bonnat was seemingly sufficient for the young artist to assimilate his teacher's drawing technique, which can be observed in this sheet.[3] After laying in the figure with broad strokes, he hatched the shadows, then stumped them to create shading. He rendered the back of the chair on which his subject is leaning by rubbing away the pigment with an eraser, a procedure he also used for the reflections on the face and neck and for the hat-brim.

FIG 99 Henri de Toulouse-Lautrec,
Portrait of Amédée Tapié de Céleyran,
location unknown

67
Pierre-Auguste Renoir
Limoges 1841–1919 Cagnes
Gabrielle and Jean c. 1895

Black chalk, 62 × 47.2 cm
Gift of Martin Fabiani, Paris, 1956
NO. 7296
INSCRIPTION
At lower right, signed, *Renoir*
PROVENANCE
Ambroise Vollard, Paris; Martin
Fabiani, Paris.

FIG 100 Pierre-Auguste Renoir,
Gabrielle and Jean, Musée national de
l'Orangerie, Paris, Jean Walter and
Paul Guillaume Collection

FIG 101 Pierre-Auguste Renoir,
Gabrielle and Jean, location unknown

This drawing, with its gentle rendering, the black chalk pigment blending delicately into the even grain of the paper, is a preparatory sketch for a painting of Pierre-Auguste Renoir's son Jean seated on the lap of his nursemaid, Gabrielle (fig. 100).[1] The subject of the child and his nanny playing with small figures on a table would be re-used by Renoir in another picture of the same title, horizontal in format and less fluid in execution, in which the toys on the table are shown clearly, in the collection of the National Gallery of Art, Washington, D.C. In 1896, the painter produced a variation that was used for a lithograph known as *Mother and Child*.[2]

Renoir's exploration of the theme of Jean and Gabrielle had its beginnings in an almost schematic charcoal sketch, in which their positions are reversed (fig. 101). Although the baby seems younger, the composition is the same, including the nursemaid's lock of hair which droops over her forehead here and in subsequent versions.

Gabrielle Renard, a distant cousin of Renoir's wife, took devoted care of the painter's children; she quickly became one of Renoir's favourite models, and at a later date, his nurse. Little Jean, whom his father portrayed many times, would grow up to be one of the pioneers of French filmmaking.

68

JACQUES-JOSEPH TISSOT, KNOWN AS JAMES TISSOT
Nantes 1836–1902 Buillon
Study for "Young Lady in a Boat" c. 1869–70

Graphite on buff wove paper, laid
down on green wove paper,
25.3 × 24.3 cm
PURCHASED 1976
NO. 18556
INSCRIPTION
At lower right, signed, *JT*
PROVENANCE
H. Shickman Gallery, New York.

This drawing of an elegant courtesan captured in a relaxed pose is a study for *Young Lady in a Boat*, in a private collection,[1] a painting that Jacques-Joseph Tissot (known as James Tissot) showed at the 1870 Salon. A sketch for the painting, in oil on paper, came onto the art market in 1995.[2] Tissot's paintings were admired – and criticized – under Napoleon III for their hyper-realistic and attractive (one might say seductive) depictions of modern life, in a style suggestive of the eighteenth century, as evidenced by the costumes of the protagonists in his scenes of outdoor amusements. *Young Lady in a Boat* was one of the last paintings the artist produced before he left for England in 1871, fleeing the disturbances brought about by the Commune. On the basis of the title – *Adrift* – given to a photograph of the work that was published on the occasion of the Salon, Wood, following Wentworth's lead, suggests a parallel between the literal drifting of the boat and the moral laxity of its occupant.[3]

The flawless execution of the 1870 painting has its equivalent in the Ottawa drawing. The artist uses a flowing line to render the young woman's full skirt, and devotes particular attention to his subject's face, propped on a slender hand, the little finger touching the corner of her mouth. In contrast, a sheet in red chalk in the Held collection deals with the overall composition.[4]

69

HONORÉ DAUMIER

Marseille 1808–Valmondois 1879

Three Judges at a Hearing c. 1862

This drawing by Honoré Daumier takes up a theme he broached earlier in the satirical newspaper *Le Charivari*. In 1849, the paper published *Physionomie de l'Assemblée*, then, in the 25 April 1852 issue, the series *Paris qui dort* featured images of sleeping judges.[1] Another drawing, larger and more polished, which is now in a private collection, shows the same magistrates officiating at a hearing: in the centre is the presiding judge, wearing his cap of office, in conversation with the colleague at his left, while the judge at his right dozes. Despite its less finished appearance, the Ottawa drawing shows a livelier, more spontaneous use of the pen and an especially expressive rendering.

The execution of the drawing in Ottawa can be dated on formal and iconographic grounds to the same period as the sheet described above; moreover, Pantazzi has established a connection with a colour sketch from a sketchbook of 1862.[2] Several of the vignettes in this sketchbook show known compositions, including some that were probably intended for sale through the sculptor Adolphe-Victor Geoffroy-Dechaume, a friend of Daumier's.[3] Édouard Papet saw in these sketches the components of a number of pen-and-wash compositions depicting lawyers, a subject frequently treated by the artist in 1861–62 after his dismissal from *Le Charivari* in 1860. Approached from an ironic point of view, the theme of the law courts, with their judges, lawyers, and clients, occupied a considerable place in Daumier's graphic work.[4] He was very familiar with this milieu, having first encountered it while still a boy when his father sent him to work for a bailiff.[5] The subject became an ideal pretext for social criticism, allowing Daumier to dissect and caricature the attitudes of the members of the legal profession.

Pen and black ink with grey wash over graphite, 13.3 × 24.9 cm
PURCHASED 1914
NO. 812
PROVENANCE
Henri Rouart, Paris (Rouart sale, Galerie Manzi-Joyant, 16–18 December 1912, vol. II, no. 43; Wallis, London; W. Scott and Son, Montreal.

70

PIERRE BONNARD
Fontenay-aux-Roses 1867–1947 Le Cannet
Study for the Théâtre-Libre Program VERSO: *Sketches of Women* c. 1890

RECTO

VERSO

Brush, watercolour, and black ink
over graphite on wove paper,
31.7 × 21.8 cm
PURCHASED 1969
NO. 15768 r/v
PROVENANCE
Artist's stamp in black ink,
Bonnard, on both recto and verso;
Charles Terrasse, Sr. (Bonnard's
brother-in-law); Charles Terrasse,
Jr. (Bonnard's nephew); Galerie de
l'Œil, Paris.

In 1890, Pierre Bonnard drew several studies, including this sheet, for the cover of the program of the Théâtre-Libre. Using his actor friend Aurélien Lugné-Poe as an intermediary, Bonnard brought his efforts to the attention of André Antoine, the director of the avant-garde theatre, but other artists also submitted proposals, and Édouard Vuillard won the commission.[1] It should be mentioned that the artistic vision of the Nabis – the group to which Bonnard belonged – applied as much to painting, decorative art, sculpture, and literature as to graphic art and the theatre.[2]

Bonnard's study provides an eloquent example of the influence of Japanese prints in the late nineteenth century on artists such as Toulouse-Lautrec, Gauguin, and Vuillard. The Japanese influence is even more evident in Bonnard's art; his nickname among the Nabi group, whose principles were articulated by Maurice Denis in 1890, was "le Nabi très japonard."[3] Cate and Ives have both shown parallels between the wide dissemination of Japanese prints in Paris in the mid-1880s and the meteoric rise of art lithography a few years later.[4] Bonnard, who got his start as a graphic artist,[5] was not immune to the vogue. He used a variety of visual processes that tended to recapitulate traditional modes of representation, and the art he created by this method was highly decorative in nature. In the Ottawa sheet, he adopted an unusual viewpoint, and outlined forms with a heavy black line, then saturated them with pure colours. The box dominating the lower left recalls the purpose of the image but also accentuates its abstract character.

Notes

CAT. 1

1. Jacques Thuillier in *L'art en Lorraine au temps de Jacques Callot*, exh. cat., Musée des Beaux-Arts, Nancy, 1992, pp. 190–92, no. 47; Jacques Thuillier, *Jacques de Bellange*, exh. cat., Musée des Beaux-Arts, Rennes, 2001, pp. 298–99, no. 82.

2. Thuillier, *Bellange*, pp. 298–99, no. 82, and Hilliard T. Goldfarb, "Bellange," *From Fontainebleau to the Louvre: French Drawing from the Seventeenth Century*, exh. cat., The Cleveland Museum of Art, 1989, p. 29, no. 6, date the sheet to about 1616.

3. Emmanuelle Brugerolles, *Le dessin français au XVIe siècle. Dessins et miniatures des collections de l'École des beaux-arts*, exh. cat., École nationale supérieure des beaux-arts, Paris, 1994, pp. 298–300, no. 93.

CAT. 2

1. Jules Lieure, *Jacques Callot*, New York, 1969, pp. 379–402. For a detailed analysis of this series, see Daniel Ternois' entries in *Jacques Callot 1592–1635*, exh. cat., Musée historique lorrain, Nancy, 1992, pp. 215–24, nos. 137–70. See also Irène Mamczarz, "L'inspiration théâtrale dans les *Balli di Sfessania* de Jacques Callot et la commedia dell'arte," in *Jacques Callot (1592–1635). Actes du colloque*, Daniel Ternois, ed., Paris, 1993, pp. 233–60; Donald Posner, "Jacques Callot and the Dances Called *Sfessania*," *The Art Bulletin* LIX:2 (June 1977), pp. 203–16; Diane Russell, *Jacques Callot: Prints and Related Drawings*, exh. cat., National Gallery of Art, Washington, D.C., 1975, pp. 74–77, nos. 80–103; Edwin de T. Bechtel, *Jacques Callot*, New York, 1955, nos. 2–4 (for the *Funeral Book of the Queen of Spain*) and nos. 84–107 (for the *Balli* series).

2. The red chalk studies are listed in Daniel Ternois, *Jacques Callot. Catalogue complet de son œuvre dessiné*, Paris, 1962, pp. 106–10, nos. 663–728 (for the *Balli di Sfessania*). See also Victor Chan, *Rubens to Picasso: Four Centuries of Master Drawings*, exh. cat., University of Alberta, Edmonton, 1995, pp. 22–23.

3. Lieure, *Jacques Callot*, nos. 381, 386, 387, 395, and 399.

4. Mimi Cazort, acquisition report, NGC curatorial file, 13 February 1984. Lieure, *Jacques Callot*, nos. 52–69. See also John T. Spike, *Baroque Portraiture in Italy: Works from North American Collections*, exh. cat., The John and Mable Ringling Museum of Art, Sarasota, 1984, pp. 68–69, no. 13, for a summary description.

5. Lieure, *Jacques Callot*, no. 521.

CAT. 3

1. Mary Cazort Taylor, "A Drawing by Jacques Callot," *Annual Bulletin of the National Gallery of Canada*, nos. 9–10 (1967), pp. 39–40; Daniel Ternois, "Callot et son temps. Dix ans de recherches (1962–1972)," *Le pays lorrain* LIV:4 (1973), p. 244, no. 24; Daniel Ternois, "Dessins de Jacques Callot. Quelques attributions récentes," in *Jacques Callot (1592–1635). Actes du colloque*, Daniel Ternois, ed., Paris, 1993, p. 378, note 26.

2. Hilliard T. Goldfarb, "Bellange," *From Fontainebleau to the Louvre: French Drawing from the Seventeenth Century*, exh. cat., The Cleveland Museum of Art, 1989, pp. 33–34, no. 9.

3. "Antonio Tempesta," in *The Illustrated Bartsch*, New York, 1983, vol. 36, p. 202, no. 958.

4. *Jacques Callot. Actes du colloque*, pp. 362–63; and see pp. 364–69, fig. 18–22, for Daniel Ternois' discussion of the studies for *The Life of Ferdinand I of Tuscany*, *Equestrian Portrait of Louis XIII*, and *Prince of Phalsbourg*. See also Daniel Ternois, *Jacques Callot. Catalogue de son œuvre dessiné. Supplément (1962–1998)*, Paris, 1999, nos. 1484, 1485, 1487, and 1507 r/v.

CAT. 4

1. A.E. Popham and K.M. Fenwick, *European Drawings in the Collection of the National Gallery of Canada*, Toronto, 1965, no. 201.

2. Hilliard T. Goldfarb, "Bellange," *From Fontainebleau to the Louvre: French Drawing from the Seventeenth Century*, exh. cat., The Cleveland Museum of Art, 1989, pp. 105–06, no. 50.

3. Correspondence between D. Lecoeur and Richard Hemphill, NGC curatorial file, 17 December 1996.

4. See "Claude Mellan," in *Inventaire du fonds français. Graveurs du XVIIe siècle*, Bibliothèque nationale, Paris, vol. XVII, p. 192, no. 322, and Luigi Ficacci, *Claude Mellan, gli anni romani un incisore tra Vouet e Bernini*, exh. cat., Istituto Nazionale per la Grafica, Rome, 1989, p. 126, no. 3.

5. "Claude Mellan," in *Inventaire du fonds français*, vol. XVII, p. 201, no. 192. This idea was advanced by Goldfarb ("Bellange") taking up Gérard Régnier's proposal in *De Raphaël à Picasso. Dessins de la Galerie nationale du Canada*, exh. cat., Musée du Louvre, Paris, 1970.

6. Goldfarb, "Bellange," no. 50.

7. Ph. De Chennevières and A. de Montaiglon, *Abecedario de P.J. Mariette sur les arts et les artistes*, 1853–54 (reprint, Paris, 1966), vol. II, pp. 130–31.

8. As painter and manservant to Henry IV, Dumonstier resided at the Louvre from 1622; he became painter to the Duke of Orleans in 1626. *Le dessin français au XVIIe siècle*, with biographies by Philippe Jaccottet, Lausanne, 1953, pp. 141–42; Jean Adhémar, "Les dessins de Daniel Dumonstier du Cabinet des estampes," *Gazette des beaux-arts*, vol. LXXV (March 1970), pp. 129–31; Louis Dimier, *Histoire de la peinture de portrait en France au XVIe siècle*, Paris and Brussels, 1924, vol. I, p. 193. For more recent biographies, see Véronique Meyer, "Daniel Dumonstier," *Dictionary of Art*, London, 1996, pp. 387–88, and É. Bénézit, *Dictionnaire critique et documentaire des peintres, sculpteurs, dessinateurs et graveurs*, Paris, 1999, pp. 849–50.

9. For a list of these engravers, see Henri Bouchot, *Les portraits aux crayons des XVIe et XVIIe siècles conservés à la Bibliothèque nationale (1525–1646)*, Paris, 1884, pp. 91–94.

CAT. 5

1. J. Guiffrey and P. Marcel, *Inventaire général des dessins du Musée du Louvre et du Musée de Versailles. École française*, Paris, 1907–12, vol. VII, nos. 5482, 5531, and 5537; see especially Dominique Cordellier, *Dessins français du XVIIe siècle*, exh. cat., Musée du Louvre, Paris, 1984, no. 17.

2. Jean Adhémar, "Les portraits dessinés du XVIe siècle au Cabinet des estampes," *Gazette des beaux-arts*, vol. LXXXII (September–December 1973), pp. 341–47, nos. 731 and 773. This album originally belonged to Michel de Marolles, the first to ascribe the drawings to a certain "Lagneau." Sold to the king in 1677, the album became a reference for the attribution of similar drawings.

3. Cordellier, *Dessins*, p. 22.

4. See Hilliard T. Goldfarb, "Bellange," *From Fontainebleau to the Louvre: French Drawing from the Seventeenth Century*, exh. cat., The Cleveland Museum of Art, 1989, pp. 103–05, and Emmanuelle Brugerolles, *Le dessin français au XVIe siècle. Dessins et miniatures des collections de l'École des beaux-arts*, exh. cat., École nationale supérieure des beaux-arts, Paris, 1994, for a brief survey of the various hypotheses about Lagneau's identity and art.

5. Anthony Blunt, in "Georges de la Tour at the Orangerie," *The Burlington Magazine* CXIV:833 (August 1972), p. 524, note 25, fig. 9, reproduced a *Portrait of an Old Woman* wearing a turban, associated with the Lorraine school of the first half of the 17th century and similar in style to the Ottawa drawing.

CAT. 6

1. The remarks by Marcel Roethlisberger, in *Claude Lorrain: The Drawings*, Berkeley and Los Angeles, 1968, vol. I, no. 668, and

Diane Russell, in *Claude Lorrain, 1600–1682*, exh. cat., National Gallery of Art, Washington, D.C., 1982, no. 43, were repeated in Hilliard T. Goldfarb, "Bellange," *From Fontainebleau to the Louvre: French Drawing from the Seventeenth Century*, exh. cat., The Cleveland Museum of Art, 1989, p. 77, no. 34.

2. Between about 1645 and 1675, Lorrain drew copies of his painting and dated the drawings. Collected in a register entitled *Liber Veritatis* (or *Book of Truth*; British Museum, London), these sheets were intended to be an inventory of his paintings and thus prevent fraudulent copies. See Michael Kitson, *Claude Lorrain: Liber Veritatis*, London, 1978.

3. André Blum, *Les eaux-fortes de Claude Gellée*, Paris, 1923, pl. 19, in *French Master Drawings, Renaissance to Modern: A Loan Exhibition*, exh. cat., New York, Charles E. Slatkin Galleries, 1959, no. 20. The dating of the print was first undertaken by Lino Mannocci (*The Etchings of Claude Lorrain*, New Haven and London, 1988, p. 237, no. 38), who situated it about 1638–41, casting doubt on the date originally proposed by Blum.

CAT. 7

1. Diane Russell, *Claude Lorrain, 1600–1682*, exh. cat., National Gallery of Art, Washington, D.C., 1982, pp. 257–58, no. 51. The Ottawa drawing is also discussed in Marcel Roethlisberger, "Les dessins de Claude Lorrain à sujets rares," *Gazette des beaux-arts*, vol. LIX (1962), p. 164, note 8; Marcel Roethlisberger, *Claude Lorrain: The Drawings*, Berkeley and Los Angeles, 1968, no. 773; and Mimi Cazort, ed., *Master Drawings from the National Gallery of Canada*, exh. cat., National Gallery of Canada, Ottawa, 1988–89, no. 47.

2. Roethlisberger, *Claude Lorrain*, pp. 293–94, nos. 772–775. Roethlisberger also lists several other studies featuring John the Baptist, including nos. 663 and 777–80.

3. Roethlisberger, *Claude Lorrain*, no. 774; Anthony Blunt, *The French Drawings in the Collection of His Majesty the King at Windsor Castle*, Oxford, 1945, no. 44.

4. This term was first used by Roethlisberger (*Claude Lorrain*, vol. I, pp. 18–20). The Grand Manner concept was subsequently developed by Russell (*Claude Lorrain*, p. 56, note 32).

5. Russell, *Claude Lorrain*, p. 56.

6. Russell (*Claude Lorrain*, p. 56) points to the Aldobrandini chapel lunettes in particular.

7. Marco Chiarini, *Tableaux italiens. Catalogue raisonné de la collection de peinture italienne XIVe–XIXe siècles*, Grenoble, 1988, p. 38, no. 18.

CAT. 8

1. Marie-Nicole Boisclair, *Gaspard Dughet. Sa vie et son œuvre (1615–1675)*, Paris, 1986, no. 358. The Ottawa drawing has

been discussed, in particular, in Pierre Rosenberg, *French Master Drawings of the 17th and 18th Centuries in North American Collections*, exh. cat., Art Gallery of Ontario, Toronto, 1972, no. 45; Glen T. Scott, *Man and Nature: A View of the Seventeenth Century*, exh. cat., Art Gallery of Hamilton, 1980, no. 13; Boisclair, *Gaspard Dughet*, p. 279; and Marco Chiarini, *Gaspard Dughet, 1615–1675*, Paris, 1990, no. 37.

2. Boisclair, *Gaspard Dughet*, p. 63.

3. See Marco Chiarini, "Gaspard Dughet: Some Drawings Connected with Paintings," *The Burlington Magazine*, vol. CXI (December 1969), fig. 50, 52, 54, 57, and Marco Chiarini, "Gaspard Dughet. Un nouveau dessin apparenté aux gouaches de la galerie Colonna," *Annual Bulletin of the National Gallery of Canada*, no. 22 (1973), pp. 17–20. There are two drawings in the Kunstmuseum in Düsseldorf and two others in the Crocker Art Gallery in Sacramento. On the two in Sacramento, see Pierre Rosenberg, "Twenty French Drawings in Sacramento," *Master Drawings* VIII:1 (1970), pp. 31–32; see also Hilliard T. Goldfarb, "Bellange," *From Fontainebleau to the Louvre: French Drawing from the Seventeenth Century*, exh. cat., The Cleveland Museum of Art, 1989, pp. 86–87, no. 40.

4. Chiarini, "Un nouveau dessin," p. 20. This resemblance was established in Jonathan Scott, *Salvador Rosa: His Life and Time*, New Haven and London, 1995, p. 210, pl. 225.

5. For a summary of current knowledge and a concise comparison of Poussin, Dughet, and Lorrain, see Eckhart Knab, "Notes sur Claude Lorrain, Gaspard et Nicolas Poussin," *Hommage au dessin. Mélanges offerts à Roseline Bacou*, Rome, 1996, pp. 333–51; for an exhaustive study, see Eckhart Knab, "Observations about Claude, Angeluccio, Dughet and Poussin," *Master Drawings* IX:4 (1971), pp. 376–83, pl. 14a–26b.

CAT. 9

1. A.E. Popham and K.M. Fenwick, *European Drawings in the Collection of the National Gallery of Canada*, Toronto, 1965, no. 209. Other sheets from the same album numbered by Ghizzi are now held in the Courtauld Institute, London.

2. Jon Whiteley, *Ashmolean Museum: Catalogue of the Collection of Drawings*, vol. VII: *French School*, Oxford, 2000, pp. 97–99, nos. 265–336.

3. Hilliard T. Goldfarb, "Bellange," *From Fontainebleau to the Louvre: French Drawing from the Seventeenth Century*, exh. cat., The Cleveland Museum of Art, 1989, p. 176, no. 88, note 4. According to Karl T. Parker (*Catalogue of the Drawings in the Ashmolean Museum*, Oxford, 1938, pp. 185–206, no. 185), one of the sheets in the Ashmolean Museum (album no. 66) carries the same monogram, *CAV*, as the Ottawa drawing, but with a different crown. Peter Thornton (*Seventeenth-Century Interior Decoration in England, France and Holland*, New Haven and London, 1978, p. 38, fig. 44; p. 405, no. 44; p. 72, fig. 78) sees two different monograms.

4. *De Raphaël à Picasso. Dessins de la Galerie nationale du Canada*, exh. cat., Musée du Louvre, Paris, 1970, pp. 48–49, no. 41.

CAT. 10

1. Jacques Thuillier, *Vouet*, exh. cat., Galeries nationales du Grand Palais, Paris, 1990, pp. 56–57. The Ottawa drawing appears under Vouet's name in "Accessions of American and Canadian Museums," *Art Quarterly* XVIII:3 (January–March 1955), p. 307, in A.E. Popham and K.M. Fenwick, *European Drawings in the Collection of the National Gallery of Canada*, Toronto, 1965, p. 142, no. 203, and in Pierre Rosenberg, *French Master Drawings of the 17th and 18th Centuries in North American Collections*, Art Gallery of Ontario, Toronto, 1972, no. 151, as a study for the famous painting *Saturn Conquered by Venus and Hope* (1645) in the Musée des Arts Décoratifs in Bourges. Rosenberg, however, questions the connection between the Bourges canvas and the Ottawa drawing. An engraving of the painting was made by Michel Dorigny in 1646; see Thuillier, *Vouet*, no. 63.

2. Hilliard T. Goldfarb, *Richelieu: Art and Power*, exh. cat., Musée des Beaux-Arts, Montreal, 2002, p. 230. See Jennifer Montagu ("Les œuvres de jeunesse de Charles Le Brun," in *Vouet. Rencontres de l'École du Louvre*, Paris, 1992) on the influence of Simon Vouet in the early works, particularly the "thesis drawings."

3. Montagu, "Les œuvres de jeunesse," pp. 538–39; McAllister Johnson in Mimi Cazort, ed., *Master Drawings from the National Gallery of Canada*, exh. cat., National Gallery of Canada, Ottawa, 1988–89, no. 48; Barbara Brejon de Lavergnée, "New Attributions around Simon Vouet," *Master Drawings* XIII–XIV:3 (Autumn 1986), p. 348; letter, NGC curatorial file, 31 January 1984.

4. "Michel Lasne," in *Inventaire du fonds français. Graveurs du XVIIe siècle*, Bibliothèque nationale, Paris, vol. VII, p. 283, no. 748. The entire image appears in Daniel Wildenstein, "Les œuvres de Charles Le Brun d'après les gravures de son temps," *Gazette des beaux-arts*, vol. LXVI (July–August 1965), p. 53, no. 284.

5. Hilliard T. Goldfarb, "Bellange," *From Fontainebleau to the Louvre: French Drawing from the Seventeenth Century*, exh. cat., The Cleveland Museum of Art, 1989, pp. 195–98, no. 100; Maxime Préaud in Goldfarb, *Richelieu*, pp. 227–28, nos. 97–98.

6. See Emmanuelle Brugerolles, *Le dessin français au XVIIe siècle dans les collections de l'École des beaux-arts*, Paris, 2001, p. 294.

7. Goldfarb, *Richelieu*, no. 98; Jacob Bean, *15th–18th Century French Drawings in the Metropolitan Museum of Art*, New York, 1986, no. 157.

8. Cara Denison Dufour, *French Master Drawings from the Pierpont Morgan Library*, exh. cat., The Pierpont Morgan Library, New York, 1992, p. 70, no. 29.

CAT. 11

1. For a thorough analysis, see Sonia Couturier, "A *Study of Nestor and His Acolytes, after Peter Paul Rubens*, by Charles de La Fosse," *National Gallery of Canada Review*, Ottawa, vol. IV (2003).

2. Because La Fosse's signature does not appear on any minutes of the Académie for 1697–98, Gustin-Gomez ("Charles de La Fosse, 1636–1716," unpublished Ph.D. thesis, Université Paris IV Sorbonne, 2003) hypothesizes that La Fosse could have travelled to Flanders during that time and seen the Rubens *modello* there. Written communication, 3 February 2003.

3. Jo Hedley, "Toward a New Century: Charles de La Fosse as a Draftsman," *Master Drawings* XXXIX:3 (2001), p. 226.

4. See Patrick Ramade in *Grand Siècle. Peintures françaises du XVIIe siècle dans les collections publiques françaises*, exh. cat., Musée des Beaux-Arts, Montreal, 1993, p. 366, no. 131.

5. Anthony Blunt (*Art and Architecture in France 1500–1700*, New Haven, 1998, p. 258) affirms that "it is in the *Presentation of the Virgin*, dated 1682, that the full effects of his new taste appear. This picture is closer to the mature manner of Rubens and more fully Baroque in its conception than anything that had been produced in France up to this date. The pattern is ultimately Venetian and one which had already been imitated in France since the days of Vouet; but it is seen through the eyes of Rubens, who had invented variants of it which must have been known to La Fosse. Moreover, the types and the swelling draperies are in a spirit unknown in France and directly taken from Rubens." Alain Mérot (*La peinture française au XVIIe siècle*, Paris, 1994, p. 283) also points out the Venetian influences.

6. Per Bjurström, *French Drawings: Sixteenth and Seventeenth Centuries*, Stockholm, 1976, nos. 457–59; Jacob Bean, *15th–18th Century French Drawings in the Metropolitan Museum of Art*, New York, 1986, p. 133, no. 140.

7. Bjurström, *French Drawings*, p. 101, no. 57. See also Francis H. Dowley, "Three Drawings by Charles de La Fosse," *Master Drawings* II:1 (1964), pp. 50–55.

CAT. 12

1. Didier Bodart, *Rubens e l'incisione*, Rome, 1977, no. 445.

2. James Byam Shaw, *Drawings by Old Masters at Christ Church*, Oxford, 1976, p. 356, no. 1470.

3. A.E. Popham and K.M. Fenwick, *European Drawings in the Collection of the National Gallery of Canada*, Toronto, 1965, pp. 150–51, no. 213. *Ecce Homo*, pen and brown ink with wash,

20.1 × 15 cm, Skippe Collection (sale, Christie's, London, 21 November 1958, no. 291B).

4. Ph. De Chennevières and A. de Montaiglon, *Abecedario de P.J. Mariette sur les arts et les artistes*, 1853–54 (reprint, Paris, 1966), vol. III, p. 30. Lafage "so excelled in drawing that it would be unjust to refuse to rank him among those most illustrious draughtsmen who were his forerunners" [our translation].

CAT. 13

1. Gaston Duchet-Suchaux and Michel Pastoureau, *La Bible et les saints. Guide iconographique*, Paris, 1990, p. 70.

2. Jon Whiteley, *Ashmolean Museum: Catalogue of the Collection of Drawings*, vol. VII: *French School*, Oxford, 2000, p. 96, no. 264.

3. Yves Picart, *La vie et l'œuvre de Jean-Baptiste Corneille (1649–1695)*, Paris [1987], pp. 60–61.

4. It bears noting that the original drawing for this canvas is markedly different from the final work. Pierre Rosenberg and Louis-Antoine Prat, *Nicolas Poussin 1594–1665. Catalogue raisonné des dessins*, Milan, 1994, vol. I, pp. 432–33. For details concerning the Richelieu commission during Poussin's stay in Paris, see Alain Mérot, *Nicolas Poussin*, New York, 1990, pp. 122–24, no. 15.

5. Picart, *La vie et l'œuvre*, p. 30.

CAT. 14

1. This drawing was part of an 18th-century album broken up by Colnaghi, in London, in 1955–56, which contained, among other things, academic nudes dated and signed by Boullogne between 1698 and 1713. The album also included other faun studies by Coypel.

2. In a letter dated 29 July 1988 found in the conservation file of this work, Eunice Williams informs Douglas Schoenherr of her intentions: "I am preparing to reattribute this and related studies to Antoine Coypel." In fact, the attribution is independently due to Williams and to Schnapper; see *Master Drawings 1700–1890*, exh. cat., W.M. Brady & Co., Inc., New York, 1989, no. 1.

3. A.E. Popham and K.M. Fenwick, *European Drawings in the Collection of the National Gallery of Canada*, Toronto, 1965, no. 212; Jon Whiteley, *Ashmolean Museum: Catalogue of the Collection of Drawings*, vol. VII: *French School*, Oxford, 2000, p. 115, no. 339.

4. John Rupert Martin, *The Farnese Gallery*, Princeton, 1965, no. 102.

5. Antoine Schnapper, *Jean Jouvenet (1644–1717) et la peinture d'histoire à Paris*, Paris, 1974, pp. 54–55.

6. See, for example, the drawings published by Antoine Schnapper and Hélène Guicharnaud, "Louis de Boullogne," *Cahiers du dessin français*, no. 2, Paris [1986], nos. 28–30.

CAT. 15

1. Nicole Garnier, *Antoine Coypel, 1661–1722*, Paris, 1989, no. 75. See also Gérard Mabille, "Les tableaux de la Ménagerie de Versailles," *Bulletin de la Société de l'histoire de l'art français* (1975), p. 95, no. 17, fig. 4. The Ottawa drawing is listed in Garnier, *Antoine Coypel*, no. 276.

2. Garnier, *Antoine Coypel*, p. 139.

3. *Venus Frolicking in the Sea with Nymphs and Putti*, oil on canvas, 74.4 × 59.1 cm, sale, Sotheby's, New York, 28 May 1999, lot 158, current location unknown; see Garnier, *Antoine Coypel*, no. 72.

4. *Aeneas's Ships Changed into Nymphs*, 1703–06, engraving by D. Beauvais after Coypel, Bibliothèque nationale, Paris, Cabinet des estampes, Galerie du Régent, pressmark Aa 36a folio 9 (*Ite, deae pelagi*); reproduced in Garnier, *Antoine Coypel*, no. 94, fig. 272.

5. Garnier, *Antoine Coypel*, p. 19.

CAT. 16

1. Conversation with Jean-François Méjanès, curator of drawings at the Louvre, 3 December 2003.

2. Hélène Guicharnaud, "Louis de Boullogne's Drawings for the Chapel of St. Augustine in the Dome Church of the Invalides," *Master Drawings* XXXII:1 (Winter 1994), p. 3. Louis de Boullogne was assigned the Chapel of Saint Augustine; his brother Bon decorated the Chapel of Saint Ambrose, Michel Corneille designed the decoration of the Chapel of Saint Gregory (which was repainted between 1765 and 1772), and Charles Poerson contributed to the decoration of the Chapel of Saint Jerome before being replaced by Bon de Boullogne.

3. Guicharnaud, "Louis de Boullogne's Drawings," p. 12, no. 9, fig. 15; Antoine Schnapper and Hélène Guicharnaud, "Louis de Boullogne," *Cahiers du dessin français*, no. 2, Paris [1986], no. 20.

4. The engravings originally published for Jean-Joseph Granet's *Histoire de l'Hôtel royal des Invalides...* (Paris, 1736) are reproduced in Guicharnaud, "Louis de Boullogne's Drawings," p. 12, fig. 14.

5. Around 1703, Louis de Boullogne collaborated with Joseph Parrocel, Louis Galloche, Charles de La Fosse, Hilaire Olivet, and Alexandre Ubeleski in a cycle of representations of the life of Saint Augustine for the Place des Victoires refectory. This group of works has already been discussed in Antoine Schnapper, *Jean Jouvenet (1644–1717) et la peinture d'histoire à Paris*, Paris, 1974, pp. 58–59, in connection with the set in Les Invalides.

6. Hélène Guicharnaud, "La dynastie des Boullogne, peintres sous l'Ancien Régime," *L'Estampille – L'Objet d'art*, no. 281 (9 June 1994), p. 40.

7. Isabelle Julia in *Maîtres français 1550–1800. Dessins de la donation Mathias Polakovits*, exh. cat., École nationale supérieure des beaux-arts, Paris, 1989, p. 172.

CAT. 17

1. Pierre Grimal, *Dictionnaire de la mythologie grecque et romaine*, Paris, 1963, pp. 187–203.

2. Correspondence between Pierre Rosenberg and Sonia Couturier, 22 July 2003.

3. Pierre Rosenberg and Isabelle Julia, "Drawings by Pierre Jacques Cazes," *Master Drawings* XXIII–XXIV:3 (Autumn 1986), pp. 352–63.

4. See *Maîtres français 1550–1800. Dessins de la donation Mathias Polakovits*, exh. cat., École nationale supérieure des beaux-arts, Paris, 1989, pp. 172–73, no. 66.

CAT. 18

1. Antonio Tempesta, *Jerusalem Delivered II: Canto IX*, after Tasso; "Antonio Tempesta," in *The Illustrated Bartsch*, New York, 1984, vol. 37, p. 100, no. 1216.

2. Charles-Nicolas Cochin's remarks at the Académie concerning Parrocel's talent as a draughtsman are given by McAllister Johnson in Mimi Cazort, ed., *Master Drawings from the National Gallery of Canada*, exh. cat., National Gallery of Canada, Ottawa, 1988–89, p. 164, no. 51. The Ottawa drawing was first published in *European Drawings from Canadian Collections, 1500–1900*, exh. cat., National Gallery of Canada, Ottawa, 1976, no. 18.

3. *Dessins du XVIᵉ au XIXᵉ siècle de la collection du Musée des arts décoratifs de Lyon*, Lyon, 1984, p. 71.

4. Sophie Raux, *Catalogue des dessins français du XVIIIᵉ siècle de Claude Gillot à Hubert Robert*, Lille, 1995, pp. 152–54.

5. *Dessins du XVIᵉ au XIXᵉ siècle*, no. 66; *Dessins français du XVIᵉ au XVIIIᵉ siècle*, exh. cat., Musée d'Orléans, 1975, no. 83, pl. LXXVII; Raux, *Catalogue des dessins français*, no. 56. There is also a *Cavalry Scene with Parade of Musicians on Horseback* (sale, Swann, New York, 25 January 2001, no. 123).

6. Ph. De Chennevières and A. de Montaiglon, *Abecedario de P.J. Mariette sur les arts et les artistes*, 1853–54 (reprint, Paris, 1966), vol. IV, pp. 82–83.

7. Correspondence between Hélène Rihal and Sonia Couturier, 15 September 2003. I am grateful to Ms. Rihal for pointing out that the Ottawa drawing is listed in Jack-Crosby Schuman, "Charles Parrocel (1688–1752)," unpublished Ph.D. thesis, University of Washington, 1979, D.138. Hélène Rihal is currently working on a Ph.D. in art history at Université Paris I Panthéon-Sorbonne.

CAT. 19

1. All the information in this note is taken from Colin B. Bailey's "An Early Masterpiece by Boucher Rediscovered: *The Judgement of Susannah* in the National Gallery of Canada," *National Gallery of Canada Review*, Ottawa, vol. 1 (2000). His excellent analysis must be considered the most exhaustive on the subject.

2. We refer specifically to the texts of Pierre Rosenberg (*François Boucher 1703–1770*, exh. cat., Galeries nationales du Grand Palais, Paris, 1986), Beverly Schreiber Jacoby (*François Boucher's Early Development as a Draughtsman 1720–1734*, New York and London, 1986), and Françoise Joulie (*François Boucher et l'art rocaille dans les collections de l'École des beaux-arts*, exh. cat., École nationale supérieure des beaux-arts, Paris, 2003).

3. Some of these drawings are illustrated in Bailey, "An Early Masterpiece," pp. 20 and 25, and in Rosenberg, *François Boucher 1703–1770*, pp. 48–50.

4. Letter from Alastair Laing to Colin Bailey, 5 July 2000. An x-ray examination of the painting shows a pentimento in the final work, in the area of the hindquarters; the tail was originally curled backwards over the animal's back. We can observe that the fragment has the same characteristic as the final painting. It was in the light of this observation that Alastair Laing suggested the drawing could be from Boucher's hand. See Alastair Laing, *The Drawings of François Boucher*, exh. cat., The Frick Collection, The American Federation of Arts, and Scala Publishers, New York, 2003, p. 41, notes 9 and 10 for a detailed commentary on the same hypothesis. See also Joulie, *François Boucher et l'art rocaille*, pp. 76–78.

CAT. 20

1. Regina Shoolman-Slatkin (*François Boucher in North American Collections: 100 Drawings*, exh. cat., National Gallery of Art, Washington, D.C., 1973, p. 8, no. 5) records: "The drawing was discovered in 1956 by Sir Francis Watson in an album of prints and drawings in a London salesroom, and came apparently from a private English collection."

2. "Jan Saenredam," in *The Illustrated Bartsch*, New York, 1980, vol. 4, no. 22.

3. Pierrette Jean-Richard, *L'œuvre gravé de François Boucher dans la collection Edmond de Rothschild au Louvre*, Paris, 1978, pp. 69–72; on Boucher's indebtedness to Bloemaert, see Regina Shoolman-Slatkin, "Abraham Bloemaert and François Boucher: Affinity and Relationship," *Master Drawings* XIV:3 (1976).

4. For further discussion of the influence of the Italian masters on Boucher's early career, see especially Beverly Schreiber Jacoby, *François Boucher's Early Development as a Draughtsman 1720–1734*, New York and London, 1986, chap. VI, pp. 126–63.

5. This dating was first proposed by George Wildenstein in *Fragonard, aquafortiste*, Paris, 1956, fig. 1, and taken up by Marianne Roland Michel in *Aspects de Fragonard. Peintures, dessins, estampes*, exh. cat., Galerie Cailleux, Paris, 1987, no. 1.

6. *Maîtres français 1550–1800. Dessins de la donation Mathias Polakovits*, exh. cat., École nationale supérieure des beaux-arts, Paris, 1989, pp. 216–17, no. 88.

7. Emmanuelle Brugerolles in *François Boucher et l'art rocaille dans les collections de l'École des beaux-arts*, exh. cat., École nationale supérieure des beaux-arts, Paris, 2003, pp. 232–33, no. 55.

8. Schreiber Jacoby, *François Boucher's Early Development*; *Maîtres français 1550–1800*, p. 206; Perrin Stein and Mary Tavener Holmes, *Eighteenth-Century French Drawings in New York Collections*, exh. cat., The Metropolitan Museum of Art, New York, 1999, p. 118. For a recent article on Boucher's training and influences, see Françoise Joulie in *François Boucher et l'art rocaille*, pp. 76–87.

CAT. 21

1. See Pierre Rosenberg, *Michel François Dandré-Bardon (1700–1778)*, Paris, 2001, no. 28.

2. Élisabeth Launay, *Les frères Goncourt collectionneurs de dessins*, Paris, 1991, no. 65.

3. Pierre Rosenberg, *French Master Drawings of the 17th and 18th Centuries in North American Collections*, Art Gallery of Ontario, Toronto, 1972, no. 37. For a reproduction of this portrait, see *Catalogus Schilderkunst Oude Meesters*, Antwerp, 1988, p. 106, no. 787.

4. Rosenberg, *Dandré-Bardon*, pp. 7 and 16. The author attributed to Dandré-Bardon two other figure studies in black and white chalk, probably drawn as part of the same project. See sale catalogue, Sotheby's, Monaco, 5 December 1992, no. 135.

5. Rosenberg, *Dandré-Bardon*, p. 8. Daniel Chol (*Michel François Dandré-Bardon ou l'apogée de la peinture en Provence au XVIIIe siècle*, Aix-en-Provence, 1987, p. 102, no. 108) asserts that the sheets in Ottawa and the Ashmolean "confirm the talents of our artist as a decorator and stage designer, the equal of the great Venetian masters who worked in the courts of Europe" [our translation].

CAT. 22

1. Susanna Caviglia-Brunel, "Charles-Joseph Natoire (1700–1777) dessinateur: Étude critique et catalogue raisonné," 2002, no. 282 (unpublished Ph.D. thesis, Université Paris I Panthéon-Sorbonne). The Ottawa drawing was previously published in Ferdinand Boyer, "Catalogue raisonné de l'œuvre de Charles Natoire, peintre du Roi," *Bulletin des Archives de l'art français* (1949), no. 507, and in Mimi Cazort, ed., *Master Drawings from the National Gallery of Canada*, exh. cat., National Gallery of Canada, Ottawa, 1988–89, no. 52.

2. *Charles-Joseph Natoire*, exh. cat., Musée des Beaux-Arts, Troyes, 1977, p. 73, no. 28.

3. *Charles-Joseph Natoire*, p. 21.

4. *From Michelangelo to Rembrandt: Master Drawings from the Teyler Museum*, exh. cat., The Pierpont Morgan Library, New York, 1989, pp. 39–40, no. 11.

5. Colnaghi, *An Exhibition of Master Drawings*, New York, 1998, no. 9.

6. Boris Lossky, "Sources d'inspiration d'une fresque belli-fontaine: 'L'Alexandre et Roxanne' de Primatice," *Bulletin de la Société de l'histoire de l'art* (1983), pp. 21–25.

7. For the *Recueil Crozat* (vol. II), Cochin the Elder executed two engravings "after Raphael" on the same theme (pl. 36 and 36a). The second was after a red chalk drawing that is now attributed to Raffaello Santi (Albertina, Vienna). "Charles-Nicolas Cochin, père," in *Inventaire du fonds français. Graveurs du XVIIIᵉ siècle*, Bibliothèque nationale, Paris, vol. IV, p. 610, nos. 48 and 49; Erwin Mitsch, *Raphael in der Albertina: aus Anlass des 500. Geburtstages des Künstlers*, exh. cat., Albertina, Vienna, 1983, pp. 126–29, no. 42. On Natoire's copying of the Italian masters, see Perrin Stein, "Copies and Retouched Drawings by Charles-Joseph Natoire," *Master Drawings* XXXVIII:2 (Summer 2000), pp. 167–86.

8. Dominique Cordellier and Bernadette Py, *Raphaël, son atelier, ses copistes*, Paris, 1992, pp. 307–10, no. 449.

9. Nicole Garnier, *Antoine Coypel, 1661–1722*, Paris, 1989, pp. 98–99, no. 16.

CAT. 23

1. On Fragonard's practice as a copyist, see Marianne Roland Michel, *Le dessin français au XVIIIᵉ siècle*, Paris, 1987, pp. 82–84.

2. Eunice Williams, *Drawings by Fragonard in North American Collections*, exh. cat., National Gallery of Art, Washington, D.C., 1978, nos. 17–18; on the work Fragonard submitted for acceptance, see Pierre Rosenberg, *Fragonard*, exh. cat., Galeries nationales du Grand Palais, Paris, 1987, p. 211, and Jean-Pierre Cuzin, *Jean-Honoré Fragonard, Life and Work: Complete Catalogue of the Oil Paintings*, exh. cat., New York, 1988, pp. 85–89.

3. *D'après l'antique*, exh. cat., Musée du Louvre, Paris, 2001, no. 156. The Vien canvas (Musée des Beaux-Arts, Strasbourg) is one of a "whole set of paintings à la grecque which includes the famous *Marchande d'Amours* [*The Cupid Seller*] ... whose direct links with an ancient Greek painting are explained in the booklet" [our translation]. See especially the chapter entitled "L'athénienne" (pp. 337–39), on the subject of ancient tripods.

4. Williams, *Fragonard*, pp. 44–45, no. 9.

5. See *Nicolas Poussin 1594–1665*, exh. cat., Galeries nationales du Grand Palais, Paris, 1994, nos. 142 and 143.

6. A.E. Popham and K.M. Fenwick, *European Drawings in the Collection of the National Gallery of Canada*, Toronto, 1965, no. 227.

CAT. 24

1. For a recent analysis and update of the inventory of illustrations for *Orlando Furioso*, see the excellent work by Marie-Anne Dupuy-Vachey, *Fragonard et le Roland Furieux*, Paris, 2003. The Ottawa drawing is discussed on p. 388, no. 141.

2. Pierre Rosenberg, *Fragonard*, exh. cat., Galeries nationales du Grand Palais, Paris, 1987, p. 509. According to Dupuy-Vachey (*Fragonard et le Roland Furieux*, p. 23), the drawings in this series were not intended to be etched.

3. Rosenberg, *Fragonard*, p. 508.

4. Christian Michel, *Charles-Nicolas Cochin et le livre illustré au XVIIIᵉ siècle*, Geneva, 1987, nos. 148 and 155. For a commentary on the style Fragonard and Cochin used in their illustrations, see pp. 143–45.

5. Eunice Williams, *Drawings by Fragonard in North American Collections*, exh. cat., National Gallery of Art, Washington, D.C., 1978, no. 67.

6. For a recent interpretation corresponding to the passages taken from Ariosto, we refer to Dupuy-Vachey, *Fragonard et le Roland Furieux*, pp. 308, 309, and 377, no. 141.

7. Rosenberg (*Fragonard*, pp. 508–09) mentions the drawings for *Don Quixote*, which, according to Théophile Fragonard, were published in a folio edition after being acquired by an English art-lover. The work has not been located, but eight engravings by Denon, after these drawings, do exist and are today in the British Museum, London, and the Ashmolean Museum, Oxford.

CAT. 25

1. Marianne Roland Michel (*Piranèse et les Français 1740–1790*, exh. cat., Académie de France, Rome, 1976, p. 168, no. 82) cites as an example a painting in the collection of the Musée des Beaux-Arts in Caen and its pendant, both traditionally attributed to Panini.

2. According to Roland Michel (*Piranèse*, p. 168, no. 81), a watercolour by J.R. Cozens (Fitzwilliam Museum, Cambridge) shows similarities with the view depicted in *Parc à l'antique* in the Musée des Beaux-Arts in Dijon.

3. The relation between the two artists is mentioned in particular in Alan A. Tait, *Robert Adam: Drawings and Imagination*, Cambridge, 1993, "Drawing in Italy," pp. 5–38.

4. Pierre Quarré, *Un paysagiste dijonnais du XVIIIe siècle. J.-B. Lallemand 1716–1803*, exh. cat., Musée des Beaux-Arts, Dijon, Palais des États de Bourgogne, 1954, p. 7.

5. An album of 22 of these drawings by Lallemand, formerly owned by Lord Elgin, was broken up and as sold separate works in 1963. See the Thomas Agnew and Sons sale catalogue, *Rome and the Campagna: Drawings*, 1963.

6. Lallemand arrived in Rome in 1747, two years after being admitted to the Académie de Saint-Luc in Paris (Roland Michel, *Piranèse*, pp. 165 and 168).

CAT. 26

1. Thomas J. McCormick, *Charles-Louis Clérisseau and the Genesis of Neo-Classicism*, New York and Cambridge, Mass., 1990, "Clérisseau and the Adam Brothers," pp. 55–98, and Alan A. Tait, *Robert Adam: Drawings and Imagination*, Cambridge, 1993.

2. McCormick, *Clérisseau*, pp. 55 and 58. McCormick mentions the Ottawa drawing on p. 241, note 4, no. XIX. The series of arches of Pola in the Hermitage is also discussed in V.G. Shevchenko, "Triumfal'nyye arki v risunkakh Klerisso" [Triumphal Arches in the Drawings of Clérisseau], *Trudy Gosudarstvennogo Ermitazha* [Papers of the State Hermitage], vol. XXIX (2000), p. 149, note 74 in this version. We warmly thank Elena Apostolova for kindly translating the article from Russian to English.

3. McCormick, *Clérisseau*, p. 58, and p. 242, note 9.

4. In a letter dated 20 March 1978, Kate de Rothschild calls attention to Canaletto's connection to Clérisseau's work. Comments on the details can be found in William George Constable and J.G. Links, *Canaletto: Giovanni Antonio Canal, 1697–1768*, Oxford and New York, 1989, p. 603, no. 807, pl. 152; p. 620, no. 848; and p. 622, no. 856.

5. On Clérisseau's contribution to the Virginia State Capitol, see Thomas J. McCormick, "Virginia's Gallic Godfather," *Art in Virginia* 4:2 (Winter 1964), pp. 3–13, in which Catherine II's commission is also mentioned on p. 12. The Hermitage collection contains over 1,100 drawings by the French master, most acquired by the Empress in 1779.

CAT. 27

1. Mimi Cazort, ed., *Master Drawings from the National Gallery of Canada*, exh. cat., National Gallery of Canada, Ottawa, 1988–89, pp. 179–81, no. 57.

2. The engravings are reproduced in Richard Harprath, *Sankt Petersburg und Umgebung in Russischen Veduten 1753–1761*, exh. cat., Staatliche Graphische Sammlung, Munich, 1992, pp. 32–33, no. 3, and pp. 48–49, no. 8.

3. There are two views of Saint Petersburg (no. 16) and a general view of Kazan (no. 17) in the catalogue of the sale at the Hôtel Drouot, Paris, 27 November 2000. Note that another view of Kazan accompanied the two Ottawa drawings when they were put on sale on 3 April 1968 at the Palais Galliera (nos. 200–02).

4. This drawing was published in *La France et la Russie au Siècle des lumières*, Galeries nationales du Grand Palais, Paris, 1986, no. 435, p.440.

CAT. 28

1. Sale at Drouot Montaigne, Paris, estate of Madame Ulmann, 7 February 1990, no. 86.

2. For an account of Robert's stay in Rome, see Jean Cailleux, "Hubert Robert dessinateur de la Rome vivante, 1757–1765," *Actes du congrès international d'histoire de l'art*, Budapest, 1969, pp. 57–61.

3. P. Lavallée, "Au sujet de deux marques relevées sur des dessins de la Bibliothèque de l'École des beaux-arts," *Bulletin de la Société de l'histoire de l'art français* (1923), pp. 310–11.

4. Denis Diderot, *Ruines et paysages. Salons de 1767*, Paris, 1995, p. 324, no. 97, note 83; Charles Sterling, *Exposition Hubert Robert*, exh. cat., Musée de l'Orangerie, Paris, 1933, no. 45.

5. *Hubert Robert et Saint-Pétersbourg (1733–1808). Les commandes de la famille impériale et des princes russes entre 1773 et 1802*, exh. cat., Musée de Valence, 1999, p. 184.

CAT. 29

1. Since we did not have access to the catalogue raisonné by Paul Prouté, *Les eaux-fortes de Louis Moreau l'aîné, essai de catalogue* (published by the author, 1956), we consulted instead an article by Georges Wildenstein, "Sur les eaux-fortes de Moreau l'Aîné," *Gazette des beaux-arts* (1958), pp. 369–78.

2. Given that there are practically no recent sources on the work of Moreau the Elder, most of our information comes from the article by Celia Alegret in the *Grove Dictionary of Art*, New York, 1996.

CAT. 30

1. Karl T. Parker and Jacques Mathey, *Antoine Watteau. Catalogue complet de son œuvre dessiné*, Paris, 1957, p. 325, no. 655. See also Mimi Cazort, ed., *Master Drawings from the National Gallery of Canada*, exh. cat., National Gallery of Canada, Ottawa, 1988–89, no. 50; Pierre Rosenberg and Louis-Antoine Prat, *Antoine Watteau (1684–1721). Catalogue raisonné des dessins*, Paris and Milan, 1996, no. 551; Alan Wintermute, *Watteau and His World: French Drawing from 1700 to 1750*, exh. cat., The American Federation of Arts, New York, 1999, no. 33.

2. The life and classification system of this collector are discussed in Jacqueline Labbé and Lise Bicart-Sée, *La collection de dessins d'Antoine-Joseph Dezallier d'Argenville*, exh. cat., Musée du Louvre, Paris, 1996. For the Ottawa drawing, see no. 3270.

3. Émile Dacier and Albert Vuaflart, *Jean de Julienne et les graveurs de Watteau au XVIIIe siècle*, Paris, 1921–29, vol. I, p. 193.

4. "Gilles-Antoine Desmarteau," in *Inventaire du fonds français. Graveurs du XVIIe siècle*, Bibliothèque nationale, Paris, 1946, vol. VI, p. 499, no. 114.

CAT. 31

1. Marianne Roland Michel, *Le dessin français au XVIIIe siècle*, Paris, 1987, p. 22: "It is surprising to see 18th-century authors liken ink drawings to etchings; Watelet even notes in the *Encyclopédie méthodique* that some Italian artists imitate engravings with pen and ink" [our translation].

2. Bernard Populus, *Claude Gillot (1673–1722). Catalogue de l'œuvre gravé*, Paris, 1930, nos. 231–47; "Caylus," in *Inventaire du fonds français. Graveurs du XVIIIe siècle*," Bibliothèque nationale, Paris, pp. 97–100, no. 276 (1–17).

3. Sale, Hôtel Drouot, Paris, 4 June 1970, nos. 508–512.

4. Alan Wintermute, *Watteau and His World: French Drawing from 1700 to 1750*, exh. cat., The American Federation of Arts, New York, 1999, no. 50.

5. Information from NGC curatorial file. See also Mimi Cazort, ed., *Master Drawings from the National Gallery of Canada*, exh. cat., National Gallery of Canada, Ottawa, 1988–89.

6. In the preface to the catalogue of Gillot engravings, Populus (*Claude Gillot*, p. vii) stresses Gillot's debt to Netherlandish artists: "Gillot was clearly influenced by Dutch and Flemish masters such as Karel Du Jardin and Gerrit (Gerard) Dou" [our translation].

7. Sophie Raux, *Catalogue des dessins français du XVIIIe siècle de Claude Gillot à Hubert Robert*, Lille, 1995, pp. 90–91, no. 20.

CAT. 32

1. See Margaret Morgan Grasselli and Suzanne Folds McCullagh, "Review of *Nicolas Lancret 1690–1743*," *Master Drawings* XXXII:2 (Summer 1994), p. 170.

2. A.P. de Mirimonde, "Les instruments de musique chez Antoine Watteau," *Bulletin de la Société de l'histoire de l'art français* (1963), p. 49.

3. Alan Wintermute, *Watteau and His World: French Drawing from 1700 to 1750*, exh. cat., The American Federation of Arts, New York, 1999, no. 62.

4. A.P. de Mirimonde, "Plagiats et bévues en particulier dans l'iconographie musicale," *Bulletin de la Société de l'histoire de l'art français* (1971), p. 188, fig. 9 and 10.

5. Mirimonde, "Plagiats," p. 188.

6. Mary Tavener Holmes, "Nicolas Lancret," *Dictionary of Art*, London, 1996, p. 692.

CAT. 33

1. *Watteau*, exh. cat., Palais Rameau, Lille, 1889, cited in *Master Drawings 1500–1900*, Thomas Le Claire, New York, 1992, no. 29.

2. Alan Wintermute, *Watteau and His World: French Drawing from 1700 to 1750*, exh. cat., The American Federation of Arts, New York, 1999, p. 246, no. 78. For Watteau's paintings, see Margaret Morgan Grasselli and Pierre Rosenberg, *Watteau 1684–1721*, exh. cat., National Gallery of Art, Washington, D.C., 1984, nos. P.60 and P.61.

3. The link with *The Conversation* was made in *Master Drawings 1500–1900*, no. 29, reproduced in Grasselli and Rosenberg, *Watteau*, no. P.23. On the De Troy painting, see Colin Bailey, acquisition report, NGC curatorial file, 10 August 1999.

4. Wintermute, *Watteau*, no. 78. For the Louvre drawing, see Lise Duclaux, in *Dessins français du XVIIIe siècle de Watteau à Lemoyne*, exh. cat., Musée du Louvre, Paris, 1987, no. 152.

5. In "Quillard as a Draughtsman," *Master Drawings* XIX:1 (1981), pp. 27–38, Martin Eidelberg sets out to classify Quillard's drawn oeuvre, which is still poorly known. The Louvre drawing and the one from the Fundação Ricardo do Espírito Santo Silva, Lisbon, are reproduced as pl. 23 and 24.

CAT. 34

1. *François Boucher 1703–1770*, exh. cat., Galeries nationales du Grand Palais, Paris, 1986, pp. 144–46, no. 19.

2. In an attempt at dating, Rosenberg (in *François Boucher 1703–1770*, p. 145) mentions "a set of four pictures: the *Souffleuse de Savon*, the *Marchand d'Oiseaux*, the *Marchande d'Oeufs*, and *La Vendangeuse*, engraved by Daullé and published in 1748."

3. Mimi Cazort, ed., *Master Drawings from the National Gallery of Canada*, exh. cat., National Gallery of Canada, Ottawa, 1988–89, p. 167, no. 53.

4. Mimi Cazort, acquisition report, NGC curatorial file, 1983.

5. *François Boucher 1703–1770*, pp. 145–46.

CAT. 35

1. Correspondence between Denise Cailleux-Megret and the National Gallery of Canada, 28 June 1963.

2. Correspondence between Mimi Cazort and Heinz Jekel, 15 August 1985.

3. Alastair Laing, "Boucher et la pastorale peinte," *Revue de l'art*, no. 73 (1986), pp. 55–64. On the Ottawa drawing, see in particular Alastair Laing, *The Drawings of François Boucher*, exh. cat., The Frick Collection, The American Federation of Arts, and Scala Publishers, New York, 2003, no. 11.

4. *François Boucher 1703–1770*, exh. cat., Galeries nationales du Grand Palais, Paris, 1986, p. 120.

5. For a parallel between Boucher and Bloemaert, see Regina Shoolman-Slatkin, "Abraham Bloemaert and François Boucher: Affinity and Relationship," *Master Drawings* XIV:3 (1976).

CAT. 36

1. Colin B. Bailey, *The Loves of the Gods: Mythological Painting from Watteau to David*, exh. cat., Kimbell Art Museum, Fort Worth, 1992, pp. 144–49, no. 8; Nicole Garnier, *Antoine Coypel, 1661–1722*, Paris, 1989, p. 116, no. 49.

2. Regina Shoolman-Slatkin, *François Boucher in North American Collections: 100 Drawings*, exh. cat., National Gallery of Art, Washington, D.C., 1973, no. 62. The exhibition catalogue by Monika Kopplin (*Kompositionen in Halbrund: Fächerblätter aus Vier Jahrhunderten*, exh. cat., Stuttgart, Staatsgalerie Graphische Sammlung, 1984, no. 32 for the Ottawa drawing) provides an opportunity to assess several examples of designs for painted fans by the major artists of the 17th, 18th, and 19th centuries. Françoise Joulie has pointed out that Boucher produced such designs on several occasions for notable art-lovers such as the comte Tessin and the tsarina Elizabeth.

3. Jules Badin, *La manufacture de tapisserie de Beauvais*, Paris, 1909, pp. 61–62; Édith Standen in *François Boucher 1703–1770*, exh. cat., Galeries nationales du Grand Palais, Paris, 1986, pp. 31, 33, and 331.

CAT. 37

1. Denis Diderot, *Ruines et paysages. Salons de 1767*, Paris, 1995, pp. 286–90, no. 72. The current location of the gouache indicated as no. 73 in the Salon booklet is unknown.

2. On the subject of the work exhibited, McAllister Johnson (in Mimi Cazort, ed., *Master Drawings from the National Gallery of Canada*, exh. cat., National Gallery of Canada, Ottawa, 1988–89, p. 174, note 8) reports Diderot's comment that there was "at the far left, on a pedestal table, another candelabrum; on the same side, in front of it, a night-table with linens."

3. Emmanuel Bocher, *Les gravures françaises du XVIIIᵉ siècle, II. Pierre-Antoine Beaudoin*, Paris, 1875, pp. 18–19, no. 15.

4. Cazort, *Master Drawings*, pp. 171–74.

5. McAllister Johnson refers to Louis Réau in his article, "Un type d'art Pompadour, *L'offrande du coeur*," *Gazette des beaux-arts* (April 1922), pp. 213–18.

6. See the Bonhams sale catalogue, London, 30 October 2002, no. 160.

CAT. 38

1. The entire series is inventoried in Hal N. Opperman, *Jean-Baptiste Oudry*, New York, 1977, vol. II, nos. D.221–D.497. The Ottawa drawing (no. D.400) is also listed in Jean Loquin, *Catalogue raisonné de l'œuvre de Jean-Baptiste Oudry peintre du roi (1686–1755)*, Paris, vol. VI, 1912, no. 1113.

2. Opperman, *Jean-Baptiste Oudry*, vol. II, p. 684: "Two authors – Després and Genaille – have indicated that Oudry copied or paraphrased several earlier illustrated books of fables, including the design of *Virgil Solis* for the *Aesop* of 1566, and those for Barlow's *Aesop*, a French edition of which appeared in Amsterdam in 1714."

3. The first album was subsequently sold to the British Rail Pension Fund and later returned on the art market (Sotheby's, London, 3 July 1996, lot 96).

4. *J.-B. Oudry 1686–1755*, exh. cat., Galeries nationales du Grand Palais, Paris, 1982, pp. 157–65.

5. Baron Roger Portalis and Henri Beraldi, *Les graveurs du dix-huitième siècle*, Paris, 1882, p. 243.

CAT. 39

1. For a detailed analysis of the work of Charles-Nicolas Cochin in the context of 18th-century art, see Christian Michel, *Charles-Nicolas Cochin et l'art des Lumières*, Rome, 1993. On his work as an illustrator, see especially Christian Michel, *Charles-Nicolas Cochin et le livre illustré au XVIIIᵉ siècle*, Geneva, 1987.

2. See cat. 38.

3. La Fontaine, *Fables choisies et mises en vers* ("Oudry" edition), Paris, Desaint et Saillant, printed by Charles-Antoine Jombert, 1755–59, 4 vols.; "Charles-Nicolas Cochin, le Fils," in *Inventaire du fonds français. Graveurs du XVIIIᵉ siècle*, Bibliothèque nationale, Paris, vol. V, pp. 277–79; Michel, *Charles-Nicolas Cochin et le livre illustré*, pp. 375–76, no. 198.

4. "Pierre Chenu," in *Inventaire du fonds français. Graveurs du XVIIIᵉ siècle*, Bibliothèque nationale, Paris, vol. IV, pp. 277–78; p. 288, no. 41.

5. Hal N. Opperman, *Jean-Baptiste Oudry*, New York, 1977, vol. II, D.379. For the provenance, see cat. 38.

6. Marianne Roland Michel, *Le rouge et le noir. Cent dessins français de 1700 à 1850*, exh. cat., Galerie Cailleux, Paris, 1991, nos. 35–37. Mentioned in Michel, *Charles-Nicolas Cochin et le livre illustré*, p. 376; J. Girardin ("L'édition des fables de La Fontaine,"

Bulletin du bibliophile et du bibliothécaire [1913], pp. 330–47) identifies some of these drawings, but the Ottawa sheet is not among them.

7. See Roland Michel, *Le rouge et le noir*, nos. 35–37: *The Mouse Who Became a Girl* (book IX, fable VII); *The Old Man and the Three Youths* (book XI, fable VIII); *The Ass and His Masters* (book VI, fable XI).

CAT. 40

1. Edgar Munhall, *Jean-Baptiste Greuze*, exh. cat., Wadsworth Atheneum, Hartford, 1976, pp. 49–50, no. 14; Pierre Rosenberg, *The Age of Louis XV: French Painting, 1710–1774*, National Gallery of Canada, 1976, p. 49, no. 42; Colin B. Bailey, *The Age of Watteau, Chardin, and Fragonard: Masterpieces of French Genre Painting*, exh. cat., National Gallery of Canada, Ottawa, 2003, pp. 248–49, nos. 64–65.

2. For the related drawings, see Munhall, *Jean-Baptiste Greuze*, p. 50.

3. Edgar Munhall, *Greuze the Draftsman*, exh. cat., The Frick Collection, New York, 2002, pp. 52–53, no. 6.

4. Correspondence between Edgar Munhall and Sonia Couturier, 22 May 2003.

5. "Pierre-Charles Ingouf," in *Inventaire du fonds français. Graveurs du XVIIIᵉ siècle*, Bibliothèque nationale, Paris, vol. X, pp. 605–07, nos. 1–9.

6. Irina Novoselskaya in Munhall, *Greuze the Draftsman*, pp. 28–37.

CAT. 41

1. Boris Lossky, *Jean-Baptiste Le Prince*, exh. cat., Musée d'art et d'histoire, Metz, 1988, p. [8].

2. Jon Whiteley, *Ashmolean Museum: Catalogue of the Collection of Drawings*, vol. VII: *French School*, Oxford, 2000, p. 250, no. 764.

3. See Perrin Stein, "Le Prince, Diderot et le débat sur la Russie au temps des Lumières," *Revue de l'art*, no. 112 (1996), pp. 16–27; and Nathalie Volle, "Jean-Baptiste Le Prince," *Diderot et l'art de Boucher à David*, exh. cat., Musée du Louvre, Paris, 1984, pp. 521–24.

4. See especially Kimerly Rorschach, *Drawings by Jean-Baptiste Le Prince for the "Voyage en Sibérie,"* exh. cat., Rosenbach Museum, Philadelphia, 1986.

CAT. 42

1. For an overview of the career of Jean-Baptiste Huet, see Laure Hug, "Jean-Baptiste Huet ou l'art de la pastorale," *L'Estampille – L'Objet d'art*, no. 311 (1997), pp. 24–37; Laure Hug, "Recherches sur la biographie du peintre Jean-Baptiste Huet (1745–1811)," *Bulletin de la Société de l'histoire de l'art français* (1999), pp. 159–73.

2. *Diderot. Héros et martyrs. Salons de 1769, 1771, 1775, 1781*, texts by Else Marie Bukdahl, Paris, 1995, p. 189, no. 124, note 194. No. 124 includes "Several drawings, Caravans, Landscapes, Animals, some of which are painted in oil, under the same number" [our translation].

3. Mary Cazort Taylor in *De Raphaël à Picasso. Dessins de la Galerie nationale du Canada*, exh. cat., Musée du Louvre, Paris, 1970, p. 52.

4. "Jean-Baptiste Huet," in *Inventaire du fonds français. Graveurs du XVIIIᵉ siècle*, Bibliothèque nationale, Paris, vol. XI, pp. 428–30, nos. 1–10.

5. See Laure Hug, "Jean-Baptiste Huet and the Decorative Arts," *The Magazine Antiques* 162:2 (2002), pp. 54–61.

CAT. 43

1. Pierre Rosenberg and Louis-Antoine Prat, *Jacques-Louis David, 1748–1825. Catalogue raisonné des dessins*, Milan, 2002, vol. I, p. 164, and no. 154 for the Ottawa drawing. See also Ewa Lajer-Burcharth, *Necklines: The Art of Jacques-Louis David after the Terror*, New Haven, 1999, pp. 89, 93, fig. 43, pp. 100–101, 115–19, note 45.

2. Martha Tedeschi, *Great Drawings from The Art Institute of Chicago: The Harold Joachim Years 1958–1983*, New York, 1985, p. 108, no. 46.

3. Rosenberg and Prat, *Jacques-Louis David*, p. 172.

CAT. 44

1. The biographical information for this entry is taken from Neil Jeffares' inventory of 1999 in "Jacques-Antoine-Marie Lemoine (1751–1824)," *Gazette des beaux-arts* CXXXIII:1561 (February 1999), no. 188 for the Ottawa drawing. This is the most complete source of information on Lemoine to date.

2. Jeffares, "Lemoine," p. 62.

3. Jeffares, "Lemoine," nos. 5 and 167. Note that in 1963, the portrait of Napoleon, signed and dated by the artist, was included in the same sale as the Ottawa drawing, with the *Portrait de Louise Contat* (1804); Jeffares, "Lemoine," no. 169.

4. *Dictionnaire historique et biographique de la Révolution et de l'Empire (1789–1815)*, Paris, 1975 (reprint), pp. 809–10.

CAT. 45

1. For Wicar's drawings, see Margot Gordon and Marcello Aldega, *Jean-Baptiste-Joseph Wicar: Drawings*, Rome, 1995.

2. Annie Scottez in *Le chevalier Wicar. Peintre, dessinateur et collectionneur lillois*, exh. cat., Musée des Beaux-Arts, Lille, 1984, p. 44.

3. *Le chevalier Wicar*, pp. 41–44, no. 28.

4. Sotheby's, London, 23 March 1971, no. 112; Sotheby's, London, 5 November 1998, no. 48.

5. Fernand Beaucamp, *Le peintre lillois Jean-Baptiste Wicar (1762–1834). Son œuvre et son temps*, Lille, 1939, vol. II, pp. 372–73.

CAT. 46

1. Laurier Lacroix in Mimi Cazort, ed., *Master Drawings from the National Gallery of Canada*, exh. cat., National Gallery of Canada, Ottawa, 1988–89, pp. 191–92.

2. Lacroix, in Cazort, *Master Drawings*, p. 192, also remarks on an anachronism in the soldiers' uniforms.

CAT. 47

1. On this subject, we refer in particular to the detailed analysis in John F. Moffitt, "The Native American 'Sauvage' as Pictured by French Romantic Artists and Writers," *Gazette des beaux-arts* CXXXIV:1568 (1999), p. 120–24; Paul Joannides, "A Subject from Thomas Gray by Girodet," *Gazette des beaux-arts* CXXVII:1526 (1996), pp. 121–22; David Wakefield, "Chateaubriand's Atala as a Source of Inspiration in Nineteenth-Century Art," *The Burlington Magazine*, vol. CXX (January 1978), p. 20; and Hugh Honour, *The European Vision of America*, exh. cat., The Cleveland Museum of Art, 1975.

2. Moffit, "The Native American," pp. 123–24. Despite its exoticism, this interment scene shows iconographic similarities to a representation of the death of the Virgin carved on the tympanum of the south door of Strasbourg Cathedral.

3. Honour, *The European Vision*, p. 292, no. 266. Honour also situates this drawing shortly after another sheet in pen and ink that explores the theme in *Communion d'Atala* (Musée des Beaux-Arts, Besançon, no. 265).

4. McAllister Johnson in Mimi Cazort, ed., *Master Drawings from the National Gallery of Canada*, exh. cat., National Gallery of Canada, Ottawa, 1988–89, p. 195.

CAT. 48

1. See Georges Vigne, *Dessins d'Ingres. Catalogue raisonné des dessins du Musée de Montauban*, Paris, 1995, for the collection of drawings in the Musée Ingres in Montauban.

2. On the interpretation of this theme by Ingres, see Susan L. Siegfried, "Ingres's Reading: The Undoing of Narrative," *Art History* 23:5 (December 2000), pp. 666–72. For the Ottawa drawing, see in particular Patricia Condon, *Ingres: In Pursuit of Perfection, the Art of J-A-D. Ingres*, exh. cat., J.B. Speed Art Museum, Louisville, 1983, pp. 152 and 160, no. 9, and Mimi Cazort, ed., *Master Drawings from the National Gallery of Canada*, exh. cat., National Gallery of Canada, Ottawa, 1988–89, no. 63.

3. Condon, *Ingres*, p. 52.

4. Agnes Mongan, *David to Corot: French Drawings in the Fogg Art Museum*, Cambridge, Mass., 1996, nos. 213–14.

5. Condon, *Ingres*, p. 165, no. 14.

6. Condon, *Ingres*, pp. 28–30, 52–59.

7. Condon, *Ingres*, no. 13.

CAT. 49

1. Germain Bazin, *Théodore Géricault. Étude critique, documents et catalogue raisonné*, Paris, 1987, vol. IV, pp. 9, 86–87, nos. 1037–38; Bernard Noël, *Géricault*, Paris, 1991, pp. 6, 8; *Géricault*, exh. cat., Galeries nationales du Grand Palais, Paris, 1991, p. 349.

2. Philippe Grunchec, *The Grand Prix de Rome: Paintings from the École des Beaux-Arts 1797–1863*, exh. cat., International Exhibitions Foundation, Washington, D.C., 1984, pp. 65–66.

3. Lorenz Eitner, "Géricault's *Dying Paris* and the Meaning of His Romantic Classicism," *Master Drawings* I:1 (Spring 1963), p. 26. For Géricault's Italian and classical influences, see also Wheelock Whitney, *Géricault in Italy*, New Haven, 1997, "The Loves of the Gods," pp. 157–98.

4. Zoubaloff sketchbook, Louvre, Paris. Eitner, "Géricault's *Dying Paris*," p. 26, pl. 20b. However, Bazin (*Théodore Géricault*, vol. IV, p. 9) rejects the hypothesis that would have Géricault recall the Hector scene he drew around 1814.

5. Bazin, *Théodore Géricault*, vol. IV, p. 8. The author identifies only four drawings with this same leftward orientation that recall the sarcophagus scene.

6. At some point, the current verso was no doubt considered to be the primary work. The sign of wear, or folding, along the left edge suggests that the sheet was originally a recto page in a sketchbook. Conversation with Geoffrey Morrow and condition report, 26 March 2002. The Musée des Beaux-Arts de Rouen possesses a similar female nude in profile, done in graphite and wash; on the verso is a study of a warrior and a shepherd bearing the body of Paris. Bazin, *Théodore Géricault*, vol. IV, nos. 1065 and 1044; *Géricault*, exh. cat., no. 75, fig. 109 and 112.

7. On this, Eitner ("Géricault's *Dying Paris*," p. 27) states: "All the drawings for the *Dying Paris* were probably executed within a few days, at any rate within a span of time too short for a gradual maturing of style. We must conclude that the heavy-handed contour drawing of the first studies and the dashing fluency of the last sketches both lay within Géricault's range at that moment." However, Régis Michel (in *Géricault*, 1991, p. 60), argues that the female nude, because it "is more in keeping with the 'Academic ideal'," represents the outcome of the artist's formal research and is thus of a later date than the drawings comparable to *Oenone and a Nymph*.

CAT. 50

1. Lee Johnson, "The Formal Sources of Delacroix's *Barque de Dante*," *The Burlington Magazine*, vol. C (July 1958), p. 228, note 5.

2. Lee Johnson (*The Paintings of Eugène Delacroix: A Critical Catalogue 1816–1831*, Oxford, 1981, vol. I, p. 77) notes that some authors contest the drawing's authenticity.

3. Johnson, *Delacroix*, vol. I, p. 77.

4. Frank Trapp, *The Attainment of Delacroix*, Baltimore and London, 1970, pp. 25–26; James H. Rubin, "Delacroix's *Dante and Virgil* as a Romantic Manifesto: Politics and Theory in the Early 1820s," *Art Journal* 52:2 (Summer 1993), p. 50.

5. Johnson, "*Barque de Dante*," pp. 228–32.

6. Katharine Lochnan in Mimi Cazort, ed., *Master Drawings from the National Gallery of Canada*, exh. cat., National Gallery of Canada, Ottawa, 1988–89, p. 207, and Johnson, *Delacroix*, vol. I, p. 76.

CAT. 51

1. Vincent Pomarède, in *Delacroix. Les dernières années*, exh. cat., Galeries nationales du Grand Palais, Paris, 1998, p. 266. The importance of religious painting in Delacroix's oeuvre and specifically the Crucifixion theme are also discussed in Barthélémy Jobert, *Delacroix*, Paris, 1997, pp. 287–95.

2. The work dating to 1846 is now held in the Walters Art Gallery, Baltimore, while the painted sketch (1845) is in the Boijmans Van Beuningen Museum, Rotterdam. The Christ painted in 1853 is in the National Gallery, London. See also *Magdalen at the Foot of the Cross* (1829) and another *Christ on the Cross* (1848) both of smaller size, in Alfred Robaut, *L'œuvre complet de Eugène Delacroix*, Paris, 1885, nos. 296 and 1047.

3. Jean Penent (in *Eugène Delacroix, ses collaborateurs et ses élèves toulousains*, exh. cat., Musée Paul-Dupuy, Toulouse, 1992, p. 6) affirms that the *Christ on the Cross between the Two Thieves* in the Musée des Augustins was repeatedly copied by Delacroix and his students from Toulouse; Lee Johnson (*Delacroix Pastels*, New York, 1995, no. 33) argues that Delacroix no doubt saw the *Coup de lance* in 1839 during a trip to Antwerp and that it is a certain influence for the 1846 *Christ on the Cross*. For the Ottawa drawing, see in particular Jacob Bean, *Eugène Delacroix (1798–1863): Paintings, Drawings and Prints from North American Collections*, exh. cat., The Metropolitan Museum of Art, New York, 1991, no. 15, and Johnson, *Delacroix Pastels*, no. 36.

4. Correspondence between Lee Johnson and David Franklin, 12 February 2002, at the time the work was acquired (no. 40918). Robaut (*Eugène Delacroix*) lists six sheets of drawings and sketches for a *Christ on the Cross* dated 1835 (no. 367, posthumous sale). The attribution of this drawing is confirmed by Lee Johnson, as well as by Arlette Sérullaz in a conversation in March 2002.

CAT. 52

1. Dewey F. Mosby, *Alexandre-Gabriel Decamps 1803–1860*, New York and London, 1977, vol. I, pp. 121, 124–25. For the Ottawa drawing, see vol. II, p. 503, no. 222.

2. Mosby, *Decamps*, vol. I, p. 110.

3. Mosby, *Decamps*, vol. II, pl. 135A (Musée Bonnat) and B (location unknown).

4. Dewey F. Mosby, "The Mature Years of Alexandre-Gabriel Decamps," *The Minneapolis Institute of Arts Bulletin*, vol. 63 (1976–77), pp. 105, 107. The Ottawa canvas is a signed and dated replica of the painting Decamps executed about 1843–45, today in the collection of the Minneapolis Institute of Arts.

CAT. 53

1. John Ingamells (*The Wallace Collection Catalogue of Pictures II: French Nineteenth Century*, London, 1986, p. 54) mentions the existence of another painted version at the Walters Art Gallery in Baltimore (see William R. Johnston, *The Nineteenth Century Paintings in the Walters Art Gallery*, Baltimore, 1982, p. 97) and a drawing measuring 28 × 31.5 cm (larger than the sheet in Ottawa), sold at the Hôtel Drouot on 23 November 1971 [1970].

2. On this topic, we refer to Albert Boime's exhaustive analysis (*Thomas Couture and the Eclectic Vision*, New Haven and London, 1980, pp. 115–28), which also makes a connection with *The Love of Gold*, painted in 1843.

3. Boime (*Thomas Couture*, p. 124), quoted by McAllister Johnson in Mimi Cazort, ed., *Master Drawings from the National Gallery of Canada*, exh. cat., National Gallery of Canada, Ottawa, 1988–89, no. 67.

4. *De Delacroix à Matisse. Dessins français du Musée des Beaux-Arts d'Alger*, exh. cat., Musée du Louvre, Paris, 2003.

5. Boime, *Thomas Couture*, p. 127.

6. Boime, *Thomas Couture*, p. 115.

CAT. 54

1. The drawing in Ottawa has already been linked to another *Portrait of a Young Egyptian* with the same annotation and almost identical dimensions (26.5 × 16 cm). See *Jean-Léon Gérôme: exposition vente du 15 mars au 2 avril 1977*, Galerie de Bayser, no. 18.

2. Gerald M. Ackerman, *La vie et l'œuvre de Jean-Léon Gérôme*, Paris, 1986, no. 129.

3. *Gérôme and Goupil: Art and Enterprise*, exh. cat., Dahesh Museum of Art, New York, 2000, p. 151.

4. "Frédéric-Auguste Laguillermie," in *Inventaire du fonds français après 1800*, Bibliothèque nationale, Paris, vol. XII, p. 233, no. 68.

5. Ackerman, *Gérôme*, nos. 453–56.

6. Gleyre's influence on Gérôme is discussed by Stephen Edidin in *Gérôme and Goupil*, "Gérôme's Orientalism," pp. 110, 115, 117.

CAT. 55

1. Théodore Duret, "Courbet: graveur et illustrateur," *Gazette des beaux-arts*, Paris, 1ᵉʳ semestre (1908), pp. 427–28; Robert Fernier, *La vie et l'œuvre de Gustave Courbet. Catalogue raisonné*, Geneva, 1978, p. 298; Margret Stuffmann, "Courbet Zeichnungen," *Courbet und Deutschland*, exh. cat., Cologne, 1978, p. 348. "A wood engraving after the drawing was made to illustrate the text which the audience would be given to read to explain the pantomime," wrote Mimi Cazort (acquisition report NGC curatorial file, p. 2, 1978).

2. According to Timothy J. Clark (*Image of the People: Gustave Courbet and the Second French Republic 1848–1851*, London, 1973, p. 54), Champfleury wrote nine pantomimes between 1846 and 1851. See also Chantal Humbert, "Courbet, illustrateur de livres," *Dessins, destins. Gustave Courbet 1819–1877, Gustave Courtois 1852–1923*, exh. cat., Les amis de Gustave Courbet, Ornans, 1982, no. 21, and Stuffmann, "Courbet Zeichnungen," no. 318.

3. Clark, *Image of the People*, p. 54.

4. H. Lecomte, *Histoire des théâtres de Paris. Les Folies Nouvelles 1854–1859, 1871, 1880*, Paris, 1909, p. 60; Cazort, acquisition report, NGC, p. 2.

CAT. 56

1. Pamela D. Osler, "Gustave Moreau: Some Drawings from the Italian Sojourn," *Annual Bulletin of the National Gallery of Canada* 6:11 (1968), pp. 20–28.

2. Pierre-Louis Mathieu, *Gustave Moreau: With a Catalogue of the Finished Paintings, Watercolors and Drawings*, Boston, 1976, p. 62; Pierre-Louis Mathieu, "Hésiode et la Muse," *Gustave Moreau: symboliste*, exh. cat., Kunsthaus, Zurich, 1986, no. 10; Pierre-Louis Mathieu, *Gustave Moreau*, Paris, 1994, p. 59.

3. Geneviève Lacambre, *Gustave Moreau. Maître sorcier*, Paris, 1997, coll. "Découvertes-Gallimard," p. 38; *Gustave Moreau*, exh. cat., National Museum of Western Art, Tokyo, 1995, p. 64.

4. Mimi Cazort, ed., *Master Drawings from the National Gallery of Canada*, exh. cat., National Gallery of Canada, Ottawa, 1988–89, p. 215; see *Second Empire: Art in France under Napoleon III*, exh. cat., Philadelphia Museum of Art, 1978, p. 398.

5. Chesneau in Jean Laran and Léon Deshairs, *L'art de notre temps. Gustave Moreau, 48 planches hors-textes*, Paris, 1913, p. 37 (our translation).

CAT. 57

1. Aimée Brown Price, *Pierre Puvis de Chavannes*, exh. cat., Van Gogh Museum, Amsterdam, 1994, p. 179, nos. 96 and 100.

2. Brown Price, *Puvis de Chavannes*, pp. 178–79.

3. Douglas Druick in *Puvis de Chavannes 1824–1898*, Galeries nationales du Grand Palais, Paris, 1976, pp. 185–88 (lithograph reproduced).

4. Mimi Cazort, ed., *Master Drawings from the National Gallery of Canada*, exh. cat., National Gallery of Canada, Ottawa, 1988–89, p. 213.

5. Brown Price, *Puvis de Chavannes*, p. 180.

6. Correspondence between Aimée Brown Price and Douglas Schoenherr, 12 September 1999.

CAT. 58

1. Gabriele Forberg, *Gustave Doré: Das graphische Werk*, Munich, 1975, pp. 870–97; Henri Leblanc, *Catalogue de l'œuvre complet de Gustave Doré*, Paris, 1931, pp. 280–81.

2. Rolf Söderberg, *French Book Illustration 1880–1905*, Stockholm, 1977, p. 5.

3. Ségolène Le Men, "Manet et Doré: l'illustration du *Corbeau* de Poe," *Nouvelles de l'estampe*, no. 78 (December 1984), p. 12 and note 67. Because of the presence of these evanescent figures, the author includes the plate corresponding to the Ottawa drawing in a group containing plates 3, 14, 17, and 20. "Jacob's Dream" was published in *The Dore Bible Illustrations*, New York, 1974, p. 21.

4. Excerpted from Edgar Allan Poe, "The Raven," in the *Poems of Edgar Allan Poe*, Thomas Ollive Mabbott, ed., Belknap Press of Harvard University Press, Cambridge, Mass., 1980.

CAT. 59

1. Alec Wildenstein, *Odilon Redon. Catalogue raisonné de l'œuvre peint et dessiné*, Paris, 1995, vol. II, no. 1069; *Odilon Redon. Le souci de l'absolu*, exh. cat., Shimane Kenritsu Bijutsukan, Shimane, 2002, no. 61.

2. Stephen F. Eisenman, *The Temptation of Saint Redon: Biography, Ideology and Style in the Noirs of Odilon Redon*, Chicago, 1992, pp. 104–05.

3. Roseline Bacou, *Odilon Redon*, Geneva, 1956, vol. I, p. 78. The connection between the two works should be considered with caution, however, according to a letter from Roseline Bacou to Mary Cazort Taylor dated 21 February 1968: "It [the drawing in the Louvre] has no relation, in my opinion and that of Mr. Arï Redon, to the charcoal drawing *The Raven* ... depicting a standing woman with a raven at her feet. This black is actually much more an evocation of Poe's poem than an illustration

of Poe; it was given in usufruct to the Louvre by Madame Albert Marquet" [our translation].

4. *Le souci de l'absolu*, nos. 53–59; André Mellerio, *Odilon Redon, Les estampes – The Graphic Work, Catalogue raisonné*, San Francisco, 2001 [1913], nos. 37–43.

5. For a comparison between Doré's and Manet's illustrations, see Ségolène Le Men, "Manet et Doré: l'illustration du *Corbeau de Poe*," *Nouvelles de l'estampe*, no. 78 (December 1984).

6. This idea is suggested by Bacou in the correspondence quoted in note 3 above.

7. Eisenman, *The Temptation of Saint Redon*, p. 105.

CAT. 60

1. See Alec Wildenstein, *Odilon Redon. Catalogue raisonné de l'œuvre peint et dessiné*, Paris, 1995, pp. 112–21 and no. 971; *Odilon Redon. Le souci de l'absolu*, exh. cat., Shimane Kenritsu Bijutsukan, Shimane, 2002, no. 134.

2. Roger J. Mesley in Mimi Cazort, ed., *Master Drawings from the National Gallery of Canada*, exh. cat., National Gallery of Canada, Ottawa, 1988–89, p. 222, note 1.

3. Ted Gott, "Redon, Mellerio, Mantegna and the Melbourne 'Pegasus'," *Art Bulletin of Victoria*, no. 27 (1986), p. 52; the poem is reproduced on p. 65, note 47.

4. In 1913, Mellerio published a catalogue raisonné of Odilon Redon's engravings; see André Mellerio, *Odilon Redon, Les estampes – The Graphic Work, Catalogue raisonné*, San Francisco, 2001 for the revised edition.

5. On this subject, we refer to Vojtech Jirat-Wasiutynski, "The Charcoal Drawings of Odilon Redon," *Drawing: Masters and Methods, Raphael to Redon*, London, 1992, p. 156 (symposium).

CAT. 61

1. André and Renée Jullien, "Les campagnes de Corot, au nord de Rome (1826–1827)," *Gazette des beaux-arts* XCIX:1360–61 (1982), pp. 193–94, note 66; Peter Galassi, *Corot in Italy: Open-air Painting and the Classical Landscape Tradition*, New Haven and London, 1991, p. 167, note 62, and p. 170.

2. Galassi, *Corot in Italy*, p. 169, no. 201.

3. Vincent Pomarède in *Corot*, exh. cat., The Metropolitan Museum of Art, New York, 1996, pp. 73–78.

4. *Corot*, p. 73, note 4; Galassi, *Corot in Italy*, p. 167, note 61.

5. *Italian Landscape* (The J. Paul Getty Museum, Los Angeles, acc. no. 84.PA.78).

CAT. 62

1. Robert Hellebranth in Madeleine Fidell-Beaufort and Janine Bailly-Herzberg, *Daubigny*, Paris, 1975, pp. xxi–xxii.

2. Robert Hellebranth, *Charles-François Daubigny 1817–1878*, Morges, 1976, p. 202, no. 596 (Marseille), p. 203, no. 597 (Louvre).

CAT. 63

1. Loys Delteil, *Camille Pissarro: The Etchings and Lithographs*, catalogue raisonné, San Francisco, 1999, p. 210, no. 96.

2. *Pissarro: Camille Pissarro, 1830–1903*, exh. cat., Hayward Gallery, London, 1980, no. 141.

3. Ludovic Rodo Pissarro and Lionello Venturi, *Camille Pissarro, son art, son œuvre – 1632 illustrations*, San Francisco, 1989, no. 929.

4. A large number of these drawings are in the collection of the Ashmolean Museum in Oxford; see Richard Brettell and Christopher Lloyd, *Catalogue of Drawings by Camille Pissarro in the Ashmolean Museum*, Oxford, 1980.

5. Joachim Pissarro, *Camille Pissarro*, New York, 1993, p. 225.

CAT. 64

1. Different authors' opinions are discussed by Roger J. Mesley in Mimi Cazort, ed., *Master Drawings from the National Gallery of Canada*, exh. cat., National Gallery of Canada, Ottawa, 1988–89, p. 218, note 1. The Ottawa drawing is mentioned in Lionello Venturi, *Cézanne, son art, son œuvre – 1600 illustrations*, Paris, 1936, nos. 1632–33; Lionello Venturi, "Giunte a Cézanne," *Commentari: Rivista di critica e storia dell'arte*, Anno 2 (1951), p. 48; Adrien Chappuis, *The Drawings of Paul Cézanne: A Catalogue Raisonné*, London, 1973, vol. I, p. 266, vol. II, no. 1180; Lionello Venturi, *Cézanne*, New York, 1978, p. 104, no. 7; John Rewald, *Paul Cézanne: The Watercolours, a Catalogue Raisonné*, London, 1983, no. 264; Götz Adriani, *Paul Cézanne. Aquarelle*, Kunsthalle Tübingen, Cologne, 2002 [1984], no. 39.

2. Mesley in Cazort, *Master Drawings*, p. 218.

3. Chappuis, *The Drawings of Paul Cézanne*, p. [15].

CAT. 65

1. Aside from the sheets from three notebooks (nos. 1, 16, and 19) in the Bibliothèque nationale in Paris, other drawings are now dispersed in a large number of private and public collections, including those of the Louvre and the Nationalmuseum in Stockholm. The parallel between some of these sheets and the composition of the drawing in Ottawa was first established by Theodore Reff, *Degas: The Artist's Mind*, New York, 1976, p. 45, note 26, and Jean Sutherland Boggs, *Degas at the Races*, exh. cat., National Gallery of Art, Washington, D.C., 1998, p. 26, note 34. See also François Daulte, *French Watercolors of the 19th Century*, New York, 1969, pp. 94–95; Fiorella Minervino and Jacques Lasaigne, *Tout l'œuvre peint de Degas*, Paris, 1974, no. 101; and Paul-André Lemoisne, *Degas et son œuvre*, Paris, 1984 [1946], no. 93.

2. Michael Pantazzi, acquisition report, NGC curatorial file, 1998.

3. Douglas Cooper, "Alexandre et le Bucéphale," in *Pastels by Edgar Degas*, New York, 1953, p. 15.

4. Reff, *Degas*, p. 45.

CAT. 66

1. Anne Roquebert in *Toulouse-Lautrec*, exh. cat., Galeries nationales du Grand Palais, Paris, 1992, p. 92. The Ottawa drawing is also mentioned in Agnes Mongan, *Henri de Toulouse-Lautrec: Portraits and Figure Studies, The Early Years*, exh. cat., Fogg Art Museum, Cambridge, Mass., 1965, no. 1; M.G. Dortu, *Toulouse-Lautrec et son œuvre*, New York, 1971, vol. V, no. D.I.908; and Gale B. Murray, *Toulouse-Lautrec: The Formative Years (1878–1891)*, Oxford, 1991, p. 235.

2. Toulouse-Lautrec's correspondence was published by Herbert D. Schimmel, *The Letters of Henri de Toulouse-Lautrec*, 1991.

3. Roquebert in *Toulouse-Lautrec*, p. 94; Murray, *Toulouse-Lautrec: The Formative Years*, p. 36.

CAT. 67

1. Colin B. Bailey, *Renoir's Portraits: Impressions of an Age*, exh. cat., National Gallery of Canada, Ottawa, 1997, no. 54 and p. 326.

2. Jean Leymarie and Michel Melot, *The Graphic Works of the Impressionists: Manet, Pissarro, Renoir, Cezanne, Sisley*, New York, 1972, no. R10.

CAT. 68

1. Nancy Rose Marshall and Malcolm Warner, *James Tissot: Victorian Life / Modern Love*, exh. cat., The American Federation of Arts, New York, 1999, p. 28, no. 3.

2. Sotheby's, London, *Victorian Pictures*, 7 June 1995, no. 141.

3. Christopher Wood, *Tissot*, Boston, 1986, p. 48: "*The Young Lady in a Boat* was published as a Salon photograph entitled *À la dérive* or *Adrift*, clearly indicating that both the boat and its lovely occupant were morally off course." The same idea was suggested by Michael J. Wentworth ("Tissot's *On the Thames, a Heron*," *The Minneapolis Institute of Arts Bulletin*, vol. LXII (1975), p. 36), who established a connection with the work of Courbet.

4. Information taken from *Gernsheim Corpus Photographicum of Drawings*.

CAT. 69

1. Michael Pantazzi in *Daumier, 1808–1879*, exh. cat., National Gallery of Canada, Ottawa, 1999, p. 369.

2. Pantazzi in *Daumier, 1808–1879*, p. 368, nos. 217–18.

3. Édouard Papet in *Daumier, 1808–1879*, p. 363, no. 211.

4. Karl-Eric Maison, *Honoré Daumier: Catalogue Raisonné of the Paintings, Watercolours and Drawings*, New York, 1996 [1968], nos. 557–687. The Ottawa drawing is mentioned under no. 639.

5. See *Daumier, 1808–1879*, p. 544.

CAT. 70

1. George L. Mauner, *The Nabis: Their History and Their Art 1888–1896*, New York, 1978, p. 44; Colta Ives, "City Life: Public Entertainment," in *Pierre Bonnard: The Graphic Art*, exh. cat., The Metropolitan Museum of Art, New York, 1989, p. 97. See also *The Time of the Nabis*, exh. cat., Musée des Beaux-Arts, Montreal, 1998, p. 90, no. 4.

2. Guy Cogeval in *The Time of the Nabis*, p. 12.

3. Mauner, *The Nabis*, p. 36; see also Colta Feller Ives, "The Great Wave: Translation from the Japanese," *Artnews* 74:3 (March 1975), p. 33.

4. Phillip Dennis Cate, "The Japanese Woodcut and the Flowering of French Color Printmaking," *Artnews* 74:3 (March 1975), pp. 27–29, and Ives, "The Great Wave," pp. 30–35.

5. Ives ("City Life," pp. 93–94) mentions the poster Bonnard created for France-Champagne in 1889.

WORKS IN THE EXHIBITION

The 17th Century — Italian Influence and Northern Spirit

1 Jacques Bellange, *Saint John the Baptist Preaching* (no. 15770)

2 Jacques Callot, *Figure Studies Based on Commedia dell'arte Characters*; verso: *Sketch of an Escutcheon for the Funeral Ceremonies of Margaret of Austria, Queen of Spain* (no. 28440 r/v)

3 Studio of Jacques Callot, *Study of a Rearing Horse* (no. 14836)

4 Daniel Dumonstier, *Portrait of an Ecclesiastic Wearing a Scarlet Biretta* (no. 6555)

5 Nicolas Lagneau, *Portrait of an Old Woman* (no. 6560)

6 Claude Gellée, called Lorrain, *Landscape with Trees, Figures, and Cattle* (no. 16720)

7 Claude Gellée, called Lorrain *Landscape with Saint John the Baptist Preaching* (no. 4556)

8 Gaspard Dughet, *Rocky Landscape*, c. 1665 (no. 14690)

9 Jean Cotelle I, *Design for a Ceiling Decoration* (no. 4442)

The 17th and 18th Centuries — The Academic Tradition

10 Charles Le Brun, *Study for "Fame" for an Allegorical Composition in Honour of Cardinal de Richelieu* (no. 6318)

11 Charles de La Fosse, *Study of Nestor and His Associates, after Peter Paul Rubens* (no. 40610)

12 Raymond de La Fage, *Ecce Homo* (no. 282)

13 Jean-Baptiste Corneille, *Moses and the Burning Bush* (no. 40965)

14 Antoine Coypel, *A Faun Seated on a Balustrade* (no. 6827)

15 Antoine Coypel, *Torso of a Female Nude: Study for "The Triumph of Venus"* (no. 28313)

16 Pierre-Jacques Cazes, *The Consecration of Saint Augustine* (no. 28189)

17 Pierre-Jacques Cazes, *Hercules and the Tunic of Nessus* (no. 41190)

18 Charles Parrocel, *Battle Scene* (no. 18969)

19 François Boucher, *Preparatory Study for "The Judgement of Susannah"* (no. 38550)

20 François Boucher, *An Angel Bringing Food to a Hermit* (no. 6888)

The 18th Century — Gallant Subjects and Genre Scenes

The 18th and 19th Centuries — Neoclassicism and Romanticism

The 19th Century — New Perspectives